GLOBAL PERSPECTIVES ON THE REFORMATION: INTERACTIONS BETWEEN THEOLOGY, POLITICS AND ECONOMICS

DOCUMENTATION 61/2016

Global Perspectives on the Reformation: Interactions between Theology, Politics and Economics

Edited by
Anne Burghardt and Simone Sinn

LWF Documentation 61

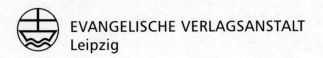

EVANGELISCHE VERLAGSANSTALT
Leipzig

Bibliographic information published by the German National Library

The *Deutsche Nationalbibliothek* lists this publication in the
Deutsche Nationalbibliografie; detailed bibliographic data are
available on the internet at http://dnd.dnd.de

This book was printed on FSC-certified paper

Cover: (Creative commons)

Editorial assistance: Department for Theology and Public Witness
Layout: Department for Theology and Public Witness
Design: LWF-Office for Communication Services

Printing and Binding: druckhaus köthen GmbH & Co. KG

Published by Evangelische Verlangsanstalt GmbH, Leipzig, Germany, under the auspices of
The Lutheran World Federation
150, rte de Ferney, PO Box 2100
CH-1211 Geneva 2, Switzerland

ISBN 978-3-374-04840-3
www.eva-leipzig.de

Parallel edition in German

CONTENTS

THEOLOGY AND LIFE IN ABUNDANCE

PREFACE

Kaisamari Hintikka

With a passion for the church and for the world—this is one of the visions driving The Lutheran World Federation. The commitment to serve both the church and the world has cut across the programs, study processes, events and conferences organized and initiated by the LWF within the framework of commemorating the 500th Anniversary of the Lutheran Reformation. The conference, "Global Perspectives on the Reformation: Interactions between Theology, Politics and Economics," held from 28 October to 1 November 2015 in Windhoek, Namibia, was one of the main events to launch the three-year core period of the Reformation Anniversary, 2015–2017. The conference brought together over seventy scholars from all parts of the LWF communion, thus offering a truly global forum for discerning the impact of the Reformation on church and society. Discussing the interaction between theological thinking, politics and economics in the different twenty-first-century contexts was motivated by the question, How do we better serve the church and the world?

Through Bible studies, plenary presentations and workshops the discourse evolved from the distinction between church and state to an increasing emphasis on the role of the citizen. In close relationship to this, the cohesion between justification and justice was explored together with the question how understanding the deep meaning of justification can liberate people and empower them for service to the neighbor and to advocate against attitudes and policies that are incompatible with the gospel. Specific attention was paid to how the global economic system and its focus on the notion of a self-regulating market affect people's lives and planet earth. The discussions on sustainable and just societies and the "good life" included workshops on gender justice, interreligious relations and theological education.

The conference participants adopted a message which affirms that all three fields—theology, politics and economics—have potential for social transformation toward a world of abundant life for all (Jn 10:10). Four core features of transformative theology that inform and are informed by political and economic realities were identified: transformative theology should be contextual, critical, creative and concrete. In this sense, transformative theology requires and enables looking with new eyes at today's realities and questioning certainties in the light of the liberating Word of God.

This publication includes a selection of papers and Bible studies that were presented during the conference in Windhoek. Hopefully they will provide helpful insights into the interaction between theology, politics and economics and encourage discussions in churches and theological institutions as we journey on our way of on-going reformation.

Global Perspectives on the Reformation

Martin Junge

Introduction

When we began preparing for the 500th Anniversary of the Reformation we pledged to observe three principles: we would emphasize the global nature and presence of the Reformation; we would observe ecumenical sensitivity in our approach by not revisiting old disputes as if nothing had changed in 500 years, but to acknowledge the fruits of our ecumenical engagement; and we would look forward, emphasizing the ongoing power of the gospel and its ongoing promise for this world.

How does the core message of the Lutheran Reformation, according to which it is not because of who we are and what we do, but because of who God is and what God does that we receive the gift of forgiveness, life and freedom, speak to us today? What transformation does it trigger? What wounds, injustices and oppression does it address?

Does the Core Message of the Reformation have any Meaning Today?

When discussing the fruits of the Reformation in today's world we have to be cautious with our approach and not to assume too much. The theme "Global Perspectives on the Reformation," and particularly its subtheme, "Interactions between Theology, Politics and Economics," is ambitious. It presupposes that the theological insight of the Lutheran Reformation has implications far beyond the realm of the church and speaks to the political and economic realms.

Is it really so, or is this merely wishful thinking? The core message and cornerstone of Lutheran theology is the doctrine of justification by faith alone, and Luther's personal struggle to find a gracious God led him to rediscover God's grace. Yet, what do people wrestle with today? Do all people, all over the world, wrestle with the same issues at the same time? Do people in the same village or society wrestle with the same questions? Does a woman in a patriarchal society struggle with the same questions as a man in that society? Do indigenous populations deal with existential questions in the same way as other sections of the population? Do we really believe that young people have the same questions concerning life, joy, hope, death, fullness and transcendence as the generation born in the early 1960s? What unleashes existential anxiety today?

The doctrine of justification by faith alone was a theological insight that developed an immense dynamic and plunged an entire worldview into profound transformation. But what coordinates determine today's worldviews? Does a religious view matter at all in a secular society? Is there **one** prevailing system of coordinates that orders people's worldviews throughout the world? Are some of the conflicts and struggles today not precisely about the emergence of alternative coordinate systems and the attempt to overcome inherited coordinates, often experienced as alienating because they were imposed?

Finally, the sixteenth-century Reformation was readily accepted by many people in Europe at the time. Can that movement continue to retain its relevance in this "one world," with its huge complexities, its shifting centers of gravity, and its polycentric nature?

AFFIRMING THE INTERSECTIONS BETWEEN THEOLOGY, ECONOMICS AND POLITICS

The sixteenth-century Lutheran Reformation can only be explained in light of the political and economic environment in Luther's time, to which his theological insight spoke so powerfully.

We need to be careful not to romanticize and idealize the Reformation as if it had been exclusively the struggle about theological ideas and principles, doctrines and dogmas. Undoubtedly, the Reformation's insight of justification by faith alone is a deeply theological issue. The power of that insight, however, and the wave of transformation it unleashed, can only be explained against the background of the immense, complex, and demanding changes in sixteenth-century western European societies, which were transiting into a capitalist economy. At the time, the political powers—ecclesial and earthly alike—were trapped in suffocating debts (how else can we explain the commerce with indulgences?). They had to deal with emerging national identities that were gaining strength and fragmenting the hegemonic agendas of the prevailing empire and cope with a New World, "discovered" only decades before and flooding the ruined western economies with tons of silver and gold, to the detriment of artisans, peasants and workers.

It was in this environment that the theological insights of the Reformation spoke, flourished and triggered change. The Reformation was a catalyst for the change that was in the air, an impulse to reassess the difficult question of the redistribution of power. In addition, the Lutheran Reformation did not always only serve as catalyst to process important social and political questions; it also became an instrument of these struggles for power. It is quite obvious that the horrific violence that disguised itself in religious clothing and virtually halved the western European population during the decades following the Reformation was not just about theology but about hegemonic powers in a fierce dispute over space and supremacy—and faith and religion became aligned with that dispute.

This fact is of particular importance today in view of understanding (a) what the issues are today; (b) the fact that once again we see so much "religious clothing" around disputes of power, resources and supremacy; and (c) throughout the programs and activities around the 500th Anniversary of the Reformation to maintain a non-triumphalist approach. The *simul iustus et peccator* of Lutheran theology needs to be applied to the overall process of Lutheran reformation—and as Lutherans we have the theological resources to do so. There should be no place for self-justification among churches that say they live from the gift of justification by faith alone.

THE CHURCH IN THE PUBLIC SPACE

I would like to highlight another aspect before exploring some dimensions of the LWF theme and the sub-themes for the Reformation Anniversary, namely the assumption that the place of the church is in the public sphere.

It has been hard for me to understand the theological tradition that confines faith to the inner sphere of the individual. The anxiety in regard to the public space is difficult to understand in view of the fact that God, incarnated in Jesus Christ, mainly simply wandered around in the public sphere to bring the good news of salvation. How can we explain a withdrawal into the private sphere in light of the biblical account of the disciples overcoming their fear and introversion when they were visited by the risen Lord and how that encounter pushed them into the public realm?

The Lutheran Reformation was such a step into the public realm. Today scholars agree that Luther's key insight about justification by faith alone had been discovered and articulated years before it unleashed its explosive power in 1517. Some scholars argue that already in Luther's lectures on the Psalms one can clearly identify this insight. Others date it later, during his lectures on the letter of Paul to the Romans. However, all agree that the Reformation's insight had been there for some years already, and that Luther may have already taught it to his students for several years without any major consequences, mass movements and social, political and religious upheaval, and that no authorities had related to it nor emperor dealt with it. What provoked the change? How did it develop its transformative power?

I believe it was Luther's pastoral and diaconal concern for people that made the difference. Indeed, while one may argue whether the Ninety-Five Theses were actually nailed to the Castle Church's door or not, it was clearly Luther's concern about ordinary people putting their trust in a financial transaction as a means to secure their eternal life (indulgences) that compelled him to go to the public, to protest, critique, and to advise on the basis of what he had recognized as the truth of the gospel. It was his agony about people being so fundamentally misled, to the point of putting their trust in a coin, which provoked him to speak out publicly. It was his prophetic anger about the church of his time bluntly turning something the Scriptures teach is a free gift into a commodity. It was Luther's diaconal concern that motivated him to offer his theological insight—developed in prayer life and academic research—to the noisy and messy world of the ordinary people. Luther saw these people—some of whom were extremly poor and marginalized—offering their small coins for a bit of peace in their hearts, at least for life after death, given that life on earth was just a torment and nightmare with no end in sight.

Academic research as a resource for ordinary people struggling with existential questions and the combination of rigorous scholarly work and compassionate witness—this is how I believe the balance between academia and the mission of the church to have been ideally struck during the Reformation. It is my hope that the vision for such a balance, which holds together and embraces the tension resulting from these two poles, will prevail in the many discussions among churches around the world today.

SOME PERSPECTIVES ON THE THEOLOGICAL INSIGHTS OF THE REFORMATION

How can we accomplish a contemporary approach to the Reformation Anniversary that unpacks the power of the Reformation's insights for today's world? In light of this question, the LWF came up with a thematic approach that helps to connect the Reformation insights with the current issues and challenges that characterize many of our shared realities today. This thematic approach will hopefully be useful also beyond the Reformation Anniversary by inviting churches to reflect on themselves and on their contexts.

The LWF adopted "Liberated by God's Grace" as the main theme for the 500th Anniversary of the Reformation. The following three subthemes help to explicate different aspects of the main theme: Salvation—not for Sale; Human Beings—not for Sale; Creation—not for Sale

What "not for sale" means will probably be immediately clear. It relates to the prophetic opposition that Luther brought to public attention in the sixteenth century by posting his Ninety-Five Theses. At the time, he objected to a gift, offered by God for free, becoming a commodity controlled by the religious power of the time, the church.

This general protest has lost none of its vitality and pertinence: it is about opposing the marketing of gifts that by their very nature are non-marketable and must never become the object of monetary transactions. Luther's prophetic "No!" is then illustrated at three different levels: salvation, human beings and creation.

Against marketing faith and the church

The first sub-theme—"Salvation—not for Sale"—does not revisit the argument concerning indulgences that flared up in the sixteenth century. It does, however, revisit the question of the current commodification of redemption, prosperity and life in abundance because works righteousness and marketing the benefits of salvation have today taken on completely different, yet similarly dramatic, dimensions as in the sixteenth century.

What do we mean here? First of all, it is about self-critically examining to what extent churches in the Reformation tradition proclaim the priority of grace in their preaching and witness. Legalism creeps in time and again; preconditions are set for grace, for forgiveness and salvation which, according to Reformation theology, are unconditional. Time and again it sounds as though we do need to do something after all, or that we need to fulfill certain ontological criteria without which we will be damned, excluded or stigmatized. Human beings continue to have terrible trouble to put up with God's subversion of human feelings of what is right, whereby God offers human beings the gift of redemption and thus of liberation—by grace alone. That is the meaning of the cross of Christ, which is at the very center of Reformation theology.

However, this theme also covers the many, sometimes even comical, forms of mercantile mediation of salvation that one can encounter in more recent forms of church. The marketing of despair and deep-seated fears has developed into a thriving business, as has the hope for prosperity. Under different headings, people are sold promises of salvation that are completely beyond any human power. The neoliberal market ideology is dragging the church, religion and faith onto the marketplace. It is not what is true that wins the day, but what sells and is successful. We need to contradict this in the spirit of a theology of the cross.

By daring to speak out in opposition to this, churches in the Reformation tradition make a significant contribution to taking responsibility for the one world that we share. The reason is that a world that never hears of or experiences grace must inevitably be graceless and will only seek its salvation in merciless competition, if not in a fight for survival that can only be won by a few. The one world will then very rapidly become the world of a few. Such a world is characterized by mechanisms of exclusion that leave their traces everywhere. This is confirmed by indigenous peoples, older people, children and young people, women, but by no means reflects the vision of the world's future revealed by God in Jesus Christ.

HUMAN BEINGS ARE INVIOLABLE

The second sub-theme, "Human Beings—not for Sale," is extremely pertinent: the migration of people from crisis areas to safe countries has resulted in gangs of smugglers unscrupulously turning refugees into commodities. This phenomenon is not at all new, but it now looms large in European public awareness. Similar manifestations of human trafficking exist in other areas: women channeled into prostitution networks; children and teenagers kidnapped and recruited for mercenary armies; people forced to sell their organs; young women and men working as cheap labor—if they are paid at all—in conditions of great drudgery, thereby guaranteeing the competitiveness of locations and industries or the implementation of major projects.

The extent to which Christian beliefs justify a fundamental rejection of these practices needs no further explanation. Every individual bears in themselves the *imago Dei*, the image of God, and their dignity and integrity are therefore inviolable. Being made in the image of God is a biblical motif of central importance for the way in which Christians understand what it means to be human.

Christians stand up for protecting the dignity of each and every person. There are also solid reasons for respecting human dignity in other religious and philosophical traditions. Humanity has developed political and legal instruments with which to express a claim to the universality of this consensus. These are the human rights covenants and conventions which, with the exception of very few non-signatory states, are binding on the international community.

The Reformation churches have an important part to play in that they distinguish between the domains in which God is active in the world (the "two kingdoms" doctrine). They therefore do not play off God's law against human law, or promote God's law in the sense of a theocracy. The distinction between the domains, in particular legitimizing a secular and thus public domain in dialectic tension with the spiritual domain, is one of the most important contributions of the Reformation to cultural history. Churches in the Reformation tradition can therefore certainly advocate for human rights and constantly call for them to be respected—they can even do so on the basis of their religious beliefs. Not because human rights are "holy scripture," but because the view of humankind expressed in them is in harmony with the fundamental tenets of the Christian faith. Furthermore, human rights are an effective instrument for protecting human dignity as a global obligation.

CAN OUR FREEDOM BE BOUNDLESS?

The third sub-theme, "Creation—not for Sale," addresses a dimension that is probably one of the most enormous and threatening challenges of our times. The lifestyle of a part of global population is in the process of destroying the ecological balance. Human induced climate change will significantly impact humanity's chances of survival if nothing is done to stop it.

Climate change—similarly to the financial crisis—points to a basic problem in human behavior: people now live from resources that they have to borrow from future generations or from other groups. This, in turn, is an expression of an understanding of freedom that has reached its limit. Ever since the Cartesian paradigm established itself, the understanding of freedom has focused so strongly on the individual that it has lived out this freedom in a striking lack of relationships and thus a lack of responsibility. One generation today takes it upon itself to consume the next generation's resources; certain dominant societies take it upon themselves to use up the resources of other groups and people elsewhere. Can that be freedom?

The Reformation churches have an important contribution to make in this field in that they can make proposals for coping with the huge challenge of how humankind can balance its understanding of freedom against social and environmental awareness in order to guarantee a sustainable future.

The initial accusation brought against Lutheran theology was that the message of justification undermined any ethical and moral fabric, in that God's gift of grace allegedly rendered all ethical endeavors baseless. The response of Lutheran theology and practice to this critique is a stroke of genius. First, by not going back on its beliefs it did not eliminate either God's gift of grace or the resultant freedom for the justified individual. This decision cannot be emphasized often enough. Churches in the Reformation tradition are churches of grace and freedom, both at the same time. Anyone in this tradition, who talks of justification by God's grace alone, will want to talk of freedom. Indeed, they are obliged to. Secondly, this freedom relates to the neighbor, specifically the suffering neighbor. Freedom, as given by God, is never autonomous or autistic—it is an essential element of Lutheran theology and practice; freedom, as given by God, finds its full expression in entering into—and protecting—relationships.

What Lutheran theology in the sixteenth century could not yet see, but what needs to be articulated more fully today in the spirit of an ongoing reformation, is the insight that human freedom, as given by God, will direct its relational commitment not only to the suffering neighbor but also to God's groaning creation. For that reason we absolutely need to move from an anthropocentric to an eco-centric theology, which sees God's saving work in the world as directed not only to human beings and their redemption but also to the whole of God's creation. This consistent and continued development of reformation theology is both a great challenge and a great gift.

GLOBAL NARRATIVES OF BEING LUTHERAN

The Lutheran Reformation unfolded through Martin Luther in sixteenth-century western Europe. However the narratives of being churches in the tradition of Lutheran Reformation vary. Ethiopians speak of Onesimus, the first local missionary who took the trouble and faced huge challenges in order to establish churches in the Protestant tradition. They speak with great respect about the Swedish and North American missionaries who came to them. That, rather than Wittenberg, is what makes up their own history of being churches in the Reformation tradition.

In India, Lutherans speak about Tranquebar, the port where missionaries arrived and chose to sit with those with whom nobody was supposed to sit: the Dalits. Missionaries touched the untouchables, and the untouchables understood God's path of incarnation as God's own way of escaping from being untouchably to becoming fully human, and hence touchable. What a powerful alternative narrative of Christian theology altogether. Again, their reference point, their geographical reference to what it is to be churches in the tradition of Lutheran Reformation, is not in western Europe but in India.

In May 2015, the African LWF member churches met in Marangu, Tanzania, to commemorate sixty years since they held their first meeting. The theme of their meeting was "From Marangu to Wittenberg," hence turning historical facts upside down and putting experiential facts forward:

their key experience of recognizing each other as churches in the same theological tradition stems from that first time they met in the region. This is what defines and shapes their identity.

The LWF member church in El Salvador would define its key identity markers as those stemming from their ministry during the war in the 1980s, and how that war called the church to the public space with valiant advocacy, diaconia and proclamation.

The member church in Russia would refer to the experience of holding fast to faith, celebrating clandestine worships in the woods, mostly led by brave, defiant women who passed on their faith to younger generations, even in times of harsh persecution.

These examples help to illustrate the polycentric nature of the LWF. This implies the convergence of many theological narratives, which together make up a global articulation of what it is to be church in the tradition of the Lutheran Reformation. The task of the LWF, as a global communion, is to create space for an articulation of theology that is inclusive of the many theological profiles that have evolved and to enable them to interact with one another, mutually challenging and deepening their perspectives. In doing so, the LWF member churches will once more grasp that the Reformation, which originated 500 years ago in the town of Wittenberg and which we will commemorate in 2017, has truly become a global citizen.

THEOLOGY AND POLITICS

Justification and Justice: The Relevance of Lutheran Distinctions in Church and Society

Antje Jackelén

Introduction: Public theology

> Today's challenges are no longer defined by local or national borders. They are glocal, both global and local. Borders are no longer what they used to be. That should not scare us. Because at the center of Christianity, there is a God crossing the most dramatic border of all: the one between divine and human. Transgression of borders always entails "Berührungsangst," the anxiety of touching and being touched by what is different, strange, other. As people of faith, we can live with these anxieties, remaining centered in the gospel of the incarnated Christ and open, very much open, to the world. And so, united in prayer for God's creation and the church of Jesus Christ, we say with confidence: *Veni Creator Spiritus*, Come Creator Spirit.

This was how I concluded my address to Pope Francis on my visit to Rome in 2015. Indeed, today's global challenges such as global warming, poverty, and people fleeing from the atrocities of war and terror are tremendous. Our mission as church can never be isolated from these and other challenges—that was a clear message both from the Pope and me.

If the mission of the church is "public," in the sense that it aims at the whole world, then our theology must also be public. Here we find ourselves confronted by the question, What is public theology? This question raises further questions and often leads to misunderstandings. What do we actually mean by public theology? A theology for the public? A theology in public? A theology contributing to public life? A theology to constitute a new public? Universal theology? Or, simply, theology as such?[1]

How can a Lutheran theology ever be a public theology? At first sight, the two kingdoms doctrine and its separation of state and church, justice and justification, does not encourage the direct involvement in today's common challenges. Lutherans have at times endorsed a rather passive, quietist ethics when it comes to public issues, justified with reference to the two kingdoms.

Sometimes, public theology is unwelcome, both in the church and "in the world." In the world, secularization and the declining knowledge of the Christian faith imply that many people do not understand, or do not want to understand, theological language. In Sweden, it is a permanent challenge to explain the theological rationale that is the basis of our involvement in public and political issues to which the love of Christ compels us. In the church, particularly in majority church contexts, the transition from an "authority church" to a "church from below" is not easy. It causes both fear and trembling; the sense of a lost identity or loss of religious language.

To my mind the task of interpreting public theology and the notion of the two kingdoms is even more delicate when it comes to (former) state churches, such as my own. Due to the close relationship between church and state, there was a neat division between law and gospel: the law was the business of the state, whereas the gospel was the business of the church. If the church lacks the capacity to handle both in theologically sound ways, then this takes its toll in the sense of the church's relevance and its theological language.

THE CHURCH OF SWEDEN AND ITS ROLE IN SOCIETY

In 2000, the Church of Sweden ceased to be a state church. This does not imply that state and church no longer have a relationship. A state law defines the Church of Sweden as an Evangelical Lutheran faith community, organized in congregations and dioceses. It has to be a folk church, governed by a democratic organization in cooperation with the clergy line of responsibility. According to the law, the church must operate throughout the whole country. The state assists with collecting the church tax, and contributes financially to the maintenance of the cultural heritage of the church, that is the numerous church buildings, many of which are medieval.

Membership numbers are declining and will continue to do so, while religious diversity is increasing. This is mostly due to demographic changes.

---

[1] James Haire, "Public Theology," in Jesper Svartvik and Jakob Wirén (eds), *Religious Stereotyping and Interreligious Relations* (New York: Palgrave Macmillan, 2013), 25ff.

More church members die than new ones are born. Since 2000, we have seen a continuous decline in membership, even if at a slower pace than pessimists had feared. The name "Church of Sweden," *Svenska kyrkan*, although a theological disaster, works quite well as a brand. It suggests that the Church of Sweden is the church to relate to. It will be interesting to see how long this perception will last.

In comparison, the Roman Catholic Church, which has never been national in the way in which the churches of the Reformation have been, does a better job of providing a Christian identity for people from various ethnic and cultural backgrounds than the Church of Sweden.

The Church of Sweden's economic resources are shrinking, and yet it is still a rich church compared to most others. It owns numerous buildings besides church buildings, whose maintenance takes large chunks out of its annual budget. It has many employees, which allows for many daily activities in parish houses. In most places, considerably more people take part in church activities during the week than on Sundays. While these activities allow for a wide array of programs and events, it may contribute to impoverishing Sunday worship life. The Church of Sweden offers a wide variety of activities, often planned and presided over by church employees. On the flip side there are church members who have been led to understand themselves as consumers of religious experiences and services provided by employed professionals. The church embraces them, responds to their needs and desires, but is not equally good at empowering them to live a Christian life and sending them to the world as disciples of Christ. This is worlds apart from the stewardship thinking I have encountered elsewhere. The consumer pattern is nourished by the fact that the average Swede does not feel the need to belong to a faith community in order to have a network of social security. Swedes are used to public welfare covering all of that, hence feel no need actively to contribute (apart from paying taxes) in order to sustain their local faith community.

One of the challenges is to rediscover the baptismal theology of gift and mission and another is to prepare for a situation with fewer employees and greater dependence on volunteers. A third challenge is finally to take responsibility for Christian teaching and education. In many ways, it seems that we still think that society provides a basic knowledge about the Christian faith, which can be built on in confirmation classes for example. But that has not been the case for decades.

Religion is a compulsory subject in primary and secondary schools. Students have a good grasp of the major world religions. However, religion is often represented as an historical or an exotic phenomenon (people who believe strange things, are against a lot of modern things, eat funny things at funny times, or do not eat, wear funny clothes, etc.). The conclusion that many students draw must be: faith is not normal; it is always the others (i.e., Muslim immigrants) who believe. A modern Swede is a non-believer.

Church and state as two kingdoms?

Needless to say, there are many ways to relate church and state, some of which are unfortunate. Let me briefly mention four examples of the latter: first, the alliance of church and state where the church dominates the state, as in Calvin's Geneva or sometimes medieval Catholicism. Second, the alliance of church and state where the state dominates the church, as in Constantinian Christendom and Colonial Christianity in Latin America. Third, the separation of church and state where politics are demonized and theology proclaims salvation as an escape from this evil world. Fourth and last, the separation that is often associated with the Lutheran doctrine of two kingdoms: a separation of church and state where politics is seen as free from all religious influence and, as a consequence, religious faith runs the risk of being privatized and spiritualized.[2]

No doubt, the doctrine of the two kingdoms has played a central role in our Lutheran tradition and, as we are only too well aware, it has sometimes had disastrous consequences—not least during the twentieth century, where there are examples of Lutheran churches that failed to work for justice and resist evil regimes.

As I have outlined above, there are other examples where this model of thinking has nonetheless led to a focus on the gospel as good news, but not for this world.

Therefore, there is a constant need to revisit the relationship between justice and justification, law and gospel, state and church.

The blessing and danger of Lutheran distinctions

In his commentary on Galatians, Luther elaborates on the distinction between law and gospel and connects it to the distinction between the secular government and the spiritual government.[3] Clearly, according to Luther the two belong together. They both apply to God's twofold struggle against evil: in the spiritual government through the gospel to promote salvation and in the secular government through the law in order to achieve political justice

---

[2] Walter Altmann, *Luther and Liberation: A Latin American Perspective* (Minneapolis: Fortress, 1992), 71–75.
[3] *WA* 40.I, 40:16–41:26; 392:19–393; 29.

and social order.[4] Moreover, according to Luther's thinking, the notion of the two kingdoms or realms has a pastoral dimension, enabling even the executioner or hangman to understand themselves as faithful Christians.

But how do they belong together? As my former colleague, Vítor Westhelle, of the Lutheran School of Theology at Chicago, points out, it is a rather new thing to consider the concept of the two kingdoms a "doctrine." Westhelle is very critical of the way the relationship between justification and justice has been interpreted in our tradition. He reminds us that the two kingdoms "doctrine" is a twentieth-century construction, originally coined by Franz Lau in 1933.[5] Cutting a long story (very) short, the creation of two kingdom doctrine, today a Lutheran hallmark, is perhaps not very Lutheran at all. From the beginning it was an unfortunate project, both in theological and political terms. According to Johannes Heckel,

> Luther's Doctrine of the Two Kingdoms, as it has been articulated in Protestant theology [read: German], is like an ingenuous labyrinth whose creator lost its plan in the middle of the work, so that [one] cannot find the way out.[6]

How, then, can we understand the two kingdoms today? One important thing to bear in mind is that in the New Testament, as well as in Luther's own thinking, there is ultimately only one kingdom, namely the kingdom of God. This is the kingdom that Jesus speaks of in the gospels, in sayings and parables; when sins are forgiven and when miracles are performed. This is the kingdom which, according to Paul, is the destiny of all creation. Thus, if we were to identify two kingdoms in the New Testament they are not church and state, but rather the kingdoms of God and evil.

Consequently, as Craig Nessan has argued, we make a categorical mistake when we read Luther's two kingdoms teaching as a spatial metaphor. They are not two unrelated realms, but rather two related strategies.[7] Evil is resisted in a twofold way: through proclamation of the gospel and

---

[4] Carl-Henric Grenholm, "Law and Gospel in Lutheran Ethics," in Carl-Henric Grenholm and Göran Gunner (eds), *Justification in a Post-Christian Society* (Eugene: Pickwick, 2014), 91f.

[5] Vitor Westhelle, "God and Justice: The Word and the Mask," in *Journal of Lutheran Ethics*, vol 3, no 1 (2003), 2.

[6] Johannes Heckel, "Im Irrgarten der Zwei-Reiche-Lehre: Zwei Abhandlungen zum Reichs- und Kirchenbegriff Martin Luthers," in *Theologische Existenz heute* 55 (1959), 317; English translation quoted according to Westhelle (cf. ibid.), 3.

[7] Nessan remarks that "strategy" is a constructive and dynamic translation of the German word Regimente just as the English term "regimen" suggests a strategy. Craig L Nessan, "Reappropriating Luther's Two Kingdoms," in *Lutheran Quarterly*, vol xix (2005), 311.

the establishment of a just order in society through the institutions of the state, law, education, economy, etc.[8] Hence, we have two complementing strategies for working against evil and for God's kingdom in this world.

Understood this way, the gospel strategy—justification—liberates the sinner from the preoccupation with their own self and salvation and enables them to do good works for the sake of others. The law strategy—justice—serves to order the world justly by political means.

This way of arguing comes close to Westhelle's claim that the notion of two kingdoms does not present "a particular Christian justice, a Christian alternative to the world, but the alternative of Christ in the midst of the world."[9] Thus, Westhelle provides us with an approach to the notion of two kingdoms, not as a doctrine where the church must not interfere in political matters, but as a hermeneutical principle: to know Christ is to know justice, and where justice is found, there we also find Christ.[10]

WHAT IS PUBLIC THEOLOGY?

Speaking of the public role of theology implies both the public relevance of theology and theology's responsibility to relate to the public sphere. I understand the public sphere as being constituted of a diversity of overlapping publics, such as religious institutions or organizations, academia, society at large, local and global and everything in between. The public sphere is thus marked by a differentiated relationality. Although it sounds like an abstract principle, this differentiated relationality is concretely embodied in the academic, for instance, who, at the same time, is a church member, citizen in a specific society and often also a world citizen.

The public role of theology requires continuous analysis of the surrounding world, dialogue in and with the current context of space and time, as well as skillful popularization of the results of theological research.

Public theology is not only possible but necessary—both for its own sake and for the sake of society. For its own sake, theology needs to be exposed to interdisciplinary and public discussion in order to develop and remain relevant. It is impossible to pursue critical and self-critical reflection without relating to something beyond one's own area.

For the sake of society, good solutions in many areas require cooperation between the best scientific, technological and theological knowledge

---

[8] Ibid., 306.
[9] Westhelle, op. cit. (note 5), 8.
[10] Ibid., 10.

and skills. Religion, its doctrinal expressions and its rites are robust and changeable at the same time.

Let me exemplify the public role of theology by turning to how many prophets live out their prophetic task. They present themselves as three-in-one: critic, child and clown in a single person. I think this scheme applies perfectly to public theology, too.

As a critic, theology will hold rationality in the highest regard and demand intellectual rigor and integrity, while respecting the limits of rationality and the penultimacy of all knowledge. This commitment will demand careful, daring and wise navigation between more than one set of Scyllas and Charybdises. Furthermore, a prophet is not a prophet without knowing history: as a critic, the theological prophet will have to be well acquainted with the history of ideas. As a critic, the theological prophet will also dare to use the language of sin, forgiveness and blessing and convincingly claim that sin and blessing are relevant to all discourses.

As a child, theology will never grow tired of asking why. With the hunger for life and the curiosity of a four-year-old, theology will keep the dimension of awe and wonder alive. It will also insist on asking those questions that the adult world has learned to avoid as inappropriate. In their dealings with all kinds of powers and sovereigns, theologians must remember that it took a child to point out the true transparency of the emperor's clothes. According to Jesus' teachings, it is a child who is the greatest in the reign of God (Mt 18:1-5). This is a relevant reminder for the dealings of the world. "… [J]ust as you did it to one of the least of these" (Mt 25:40) is a robust criterion also in secular ethical reasoning. How will this particular project affect the little ones of this world? What will it do for them? What will it do against them?

A clown is about good and healthy laughter. As a clown, theology's only power is the courage to look odd and to let itself be laughed at. The success of clowns is grounded in their ability to play with the categories of causation in such a way that they make everybody burst into laughter. Not unlike the epistemological ambition of postmodern thought to gain knowledge from the cracks in the pot of objective knowledge, the clown releases something through the cracks that puts an end to the serious composure of a face when it bursts into laughter. Or, maybe, the trick is an extra boost of those mirror neurons, our prerequisite for trust, empathy and thus even solidarity. Beyond words.

Clowns do embarrassing things, but they never embarrass others—they always take the embarrassment on themselves. By so doing, clowns create liberation for those who laugh at them. The best clownery always has traits of vicarious suffering by which others are liberated. Thus, it is the image of salvation that scientists and theologians along with all of humanity and the rest of creation long for.

In the role of clown, theology will not start out by explicitly speaking about God or the Holy Trinity; rather, it will start with sharing and enacting a specific culture while at the same time opening it up toward transcendence. It is an approach from below, as it were. The clown performs this approach by subtly playing with the category of causality: by doing the absolutely predictable (like stumbling and tripping) in always astonishing ways, the clown surpasses predictability in a stunning symphony of vulnerability and surprise. Causality is vigorously affirmed—in their gawkiness, clowns seem to be even more subject to the laws of nature than anybody else. Yet, the clown's radical submission to the rules of causality serves something else: it evokes in the spectator a vision that reaches beyond the limits of mechanical causality. Causality is strongly affirmed, yet opened from inside toward transcendence. This is creativity: something new emerging not by negating cause and effect but by participating in the symphony of vulnerability and surprise, finitude and freedom, fall and grace.

This approach is radically different from worldviews that build on a supposed dualism between the natural and the supernatural. Such views routinely adhere to a rigid scheme of distribution: the natural goes to science and technology and the supernatural goes to faith. Although outmoded, such views are still in use, especially in circles that have an interest in exposing the supposed irrationality of religion. The line of argument seems compelling: when the irrationality of the category of the supernatural is successfully claimed, religion and theology are automatically redundant at best, harmful at worst. The prophetic image of the clown convincingly questions these assumptions by undermining the dualism of natural and supernatural. Theology works without that dualism.

Another way of saying this is to describe the clown as an ideal figure that is deeply rooted in a clear analysis of reality. This is the clown's identity: clowns bring together playful idealism and utter realism in a way that creates liberation. In doing so, they bear Christ-like traits. It is precisely this combination of realism and idealism that maintains the human fascination with the figure of the clown.

The clown's subtle and liberating play with causality is deeply theological. In taking on the role of clown, theology bears witness to the divine: creativity is born where the seriousness of the cause–effect mechanism is trumped by liberating laughter. In other words: creativity implies a transcended cause–effect relationship such as the clown models it—not by negating the cause–effect structure of the natural but by allowing for something new to emerge out of the symphony of surprise and vulnerability. Similarly, such powerful dynamic comes to the fore when the reality of death is trumped by the great Easter laugh, the *risus paschalis*, known as an element in some late medieval traditions of Christian liturgy.

CONCLUSION

Critic, child and clown: in each of these roles, theology has something specific to offer to our common search for adequate and sustainable knowledge: knowledge that pays due attention to the twofold strategy of gospel and law and that knows how to use the key of deconstruction as a hermeneutics of the kingdom of God. When theology acts prophetically, as critic, child and clown, it will respect differences in ways that enable relationships and create environments where love can flourish.

We can find a basis for a Lutheran public theology, not by rejecting the distinction between the two kingdoms, but by revisiting it and by joining God's twofold mission of justification and justice for this world with confidence and hope.

Law and Gospel and Two Realms: Lutheran Distinctions Revisited

Bernd Oberdorfer

Religion matters. This was definitely true in sixteenth-century Europe. Rather like during the times of the first ecumenical councils in Byzantium when—so it is said—women at the market quarreled about the two natures of Christ, during the Reformation talk about religion dominated the public sphere and changed the world. The specific theological insights, based on the liberating concept of justification by grace through faith, gave theology a new relevance which, in many ways, permanently shaped society.

Discussions on the impact of Reformation theology on society have always been controversial if not ambiguous. For instance, from its very beginning the Reformation was subject to the critique that its emphasis on justification through faith alone renders human acts irrelevant, underestimates ethics, reduces persons to passive recipients, and thus destroys human dignity by no longer requiring that one is responsible for one's actions. At the same time, it has been pointed out that the Reformation enhanced the prestige of secular life. For instance, the Reformers abolished the distinction between "clergy" and "laity," claiming that there is only one status or rank in Christianity that is based on common baptism. They therefore declined a "two-tiered ethics," which restricted the "normal" Christian to the Ten Commandments, whereas monks and clergy, the "perfect" Christians, were dignified by additionally observing the *consilia evangelica*, the "evangelical counsels," i.e., poverty, chastity and obedience. Luther insisted that every Christian is liberated and challenged to practice love in everyday life, be it in the church or in the secular world. This resulted in a new esteem for the worldly professions, which were now also regarded as "vocations."

As to its historical effect, this new assessment of social life was and still is judged in very different ways. On the one hand, it has been noted that the theological quasi "upgrading" of the worldly professions implied an expansion of the "sphere of holiness." Therefore, it has been remarked that while the Reformers closed down the cloisters they instead turned the whole world into a monastery. On the other hand, exactly the same phenomenon has been interpreted as an important step toward secularization. This can be meant critically as well as affirmatively. Critics such as Charles Taylor[1] have emphasized that by evening out the difference between clergy and laity and abolishing many forms of religious life such as monastic vows, relics, processions, pilgrimage, veneration of saints etc., the Reformers sobered up the world, eliminated the specific sphere of religion, and made religion increasingly invisible because it diffused into society and eventually was indistinguishable from it. Others insisted that secularization established a world in which religion would find its proper place, precisely because it had lost its comprehensive authority and only retained responsibility for its own, intrinsically religious affairs, and that the Reformation played a significant role in this process. Thus, they claim, secularization should be appreciated by religion itself because it helped to give God what is God's and Caesar what is Caesar's.

Max Weber developed another perspective.[2] He observed that modern capitalism implied that entrepreneurs had a specific mental disposition, which was mainly found in countries under the influence of Calvinism or Calvinist Puritanism. He therefore stated that there must be a causal nexus between Calvinist theology and the mental habitus of the economic stakeholders. He found such a nexus in the Calvinist idea of the *syllogismus practicus*, i.e., the idea that the individual's eternal (pre-)destination manifests itself in their industrious, non-hedonistic attitude toward life and the resulting welfare. Although this particular nexus, as well as his respective assessment of Lutheranism, have been discussed critically, Weber's basic insight that religion shapes the individual's attitude to life and thus has an indirect, even unintended, impact on culture, politics and economics, has inspired considerable research in the social sciences and religious studies.

Thus, the question of how the Reformation influenced society, politics and the economy is a complex one. As to the historical origins, the Reformation clearly started with a critique, first of the profanation of the church and its perversion into an institution with worldly structures, interests and purposes, and, second, of the monetization of salvation evident in the selling of indulgences. Luther's insight of justification through faith alone resulted

---

[1] Cf. Charles Taylor, *A Secular Age* (Cambridge/MA: Harvard University Press, 2007).
[2] Cf. esp. Max Weber, *The Protestant Ethic and the Spirit of Capitalism*, transl. Talcott Parsons with an introduction by Anthony Giddens (London/New York: Routledge Classics, 2001).

in the explicit message that salvation is not for sale. From the beginning, the Reformation fought against the confusion between and combination of religion and economics or politics. Reformation meant returning the church to its primary and proper form and function of spreading the gospel, which the Reformers felt to be obscured by this blending of religion and politics. Clearly, they did not aim at withdrawing the church from the world. Not incidentally, in his seminal treatise "Open Letter to the Christian Nobility of the German Nation Concerning the Reform of the Christian Estate (1520)," Luther not only focused on the reform of the church but also pleaded for reforms in politics and society. He was convinced that the crisis in the church also provoked a crisis in society and that reforming the church would also impact society. In other words: by distinguishing the church from the "'world," the Reformers did not want to isolate the church from the "world" but, rather, to enable the church again to serve the "world." Reformation, thus, always implied the diagnosis of a crisis in society and the intention to change society.

Reformation meant distinction. But distinction did not mean separation or isolation. On the contrary, it meant identifying differences in order to establish relations. The most famous distinctions developed during the Lutheran Reformation are the distinction between "law and gospel" and the "two realms." In the following, I would like to show that both are intended to identify the church in its specific function, including its relations to the "world." Moreover, they are supposed to display the real dignity of the "world" in light of the gospel, and to indicate basic guidelines for a Christian way of dealing with it.

LAW AND GOSPEL

Whereas the distinction between the two realms marks the outward threshold of the church as it were, distinguishing law and gospel defines the church's inner identity. For Luther, this distinction seemed so crucial that he wrote, "Therefore, whoever knows well how to distinguish the Gospel from the Law should give thanks to God and know that he is a real theologian."[3] For Luther, the confusion between law and gospel was at the root of the Roman as well as the Anabaptist fallacy. According to him, the Roman church made the gospel a law by demanding human works as a prerequisite for salvation—but also by offering the ordinary people affordable ways to fulfill God's demand (because this made salvation look as if it were for sale). According to Luther, the Anabaptists converted the gospel into a legal code for the Christian

---

[3] Martin Luther, "Lectures on Galatians, 1535," in *LW* 26, 15.

community, thus turning salvation into a human action. In his famous autobiographical retrospective of 1545,[4] Luther recalled how he had suffered, knowing that he could never be righteous before the righteous God, until he understood that true righteousness "lives by a gift of God, namely by faith,"[5] in other words: not law but gospel.

From this basic insight follows a veritable spate of consequences, for the church as well as for how Christians perceived society. First, given that salvation is a pure gift, it cannot and need not be merited or bought. This implied a critique of the medieval system of repentance, which made absolution dependent on acts of contrition beforehand and satisfaction after. Furthermore, it included a critique of the church imposing new rules, such as fasting, on Christians without biblical legitimation, but claiming them to be indispensable for eternal salvation. This critique extended to the popular "bargains" the church offered to shorten and alleviate the Christian's way to eternal fulfillment, such as indulgences, because the logic of "bargains" would lead people to believe that salvation depends on what they pay for it. Thus, to concentrate on the preaching of the gospel required a restructuring of the church itself. As to the content of the preaching, it also required a new emphasis on freedom, because preaching the gospel means to communicate salvation as a free gift that liberates Christians from the stressful pressure of having to be agents of their own salvation.

Yet, to distinguish law and gospel does not mean to eliminate the law. Actually, within the Lutheran movement, there were some theologians, the "Antinomists," who claimed that for Christians the law has lost its relevance. But Luther strongly objected to this idea. The law would only be superfluous if we already lived in a state of perfection. We still live in a state of transition in which our certainty of being saved is always at risk of getting lost because of the lack of evidence of salvation. Thus we often fall back into our old life. We are "justified and sinners at the same time" (*simul iustus et peccator*). Therefore we are still in need of the law in its, as Lutheran dogmatics puts it, theological use" (*usus theologicus* or *elenchticus*). Here the law does not function as a way of salvation but a way to salvation. It is a reminder of our lacking perfection. It is a mirror that shows us that we still do not comply with God's will and are not able to overcome our inability ourselves. The law gives us a realistic, disenchanting picture of ourselves. We are neither what we ought to be nor what we wish to be, and we cannot make ourselves what we ought and wish to be either. The law leads us into a salutary desperation.

---

[4] Cf. Martin Luther, "Preface to the Complete Edition of Luther's Latin Writings," in *LW* 34, 323–38.

[5] Ibid., 337.

This paradox might sound like it were taken from a handbook on sado-masochism, but it is not. "Salutary desperation" does not mean pleasure in feeling pain or, even worse, God's pleasure in causing pain. The desperation is not salutary in itself, only insofar as it directs the hope to the gospel. The law, as Paul puts it in his letter to the Galatians, was "our disciplinarian until Christ came" (Gal 3:24). In other words: the law is salutary because it cuts off all human-made ways to salvation, leaving only the way God chose by sending his son.

But besides this "negative function" the law has also a positive one, which makes it relevant to social ethics. The Lutheran Reformers called it the *usus politicus*, the "political use" of the law. This use refers to the order of society. The Reformers were convinced that it is part of God's will to preserve, and sustain God's creation and to keep culture as well as nature, and thus also human societies, in good order. God's law provides orientation for individual and social life and God introduced institutions to establish, maintain and safeguard the social order based on the law. With reference to Romans 1–3, the Reformers regarded the law as being universal and thus as the binding authority for every human being. Whereas the Jews had the privilege to receive the law in a written form, all other people have the same law inscribed in their hearts. Luther therefore saw himself entitled to change the text of the Decalogue for use in his "Small Catechism." He emended all allusions to the specific context of Old Testament Israel and replaced it with general terms, such as "holiday" instead of "Sabbath." Of course, "law" then only entailed those parts of the Torah that did not particularly refer to certain cultic practices but, rather, were applicable to universal ethics.

Evidently the law can have this "political" function only because it is not the gospel. It only orientates the exterior life but does not (and is not entitled to) touch the soul. It has neither the competence nor the responsibility to spread the gospel. The law in this use is valid not exclusively for Christians, but for every human being. Luther therefore sometimes polemically reminded the Christian nobility that the Turkish sultans apparently governed their state better than they did.

With the *usus politicus* of the law we have already touched on the other basic distinction of the Lutheran Reformation, the "two realms."

THE "TWO REALMS"

The Lutheran distinction between the two realms has been called a maze or labyrinth (*Irrgarten*) because of the many different explanations. It is interesting that it was not referred to as a "doctrine" until the twentieth century. Remarkably enough, the term *Zwei-Reiche-Lehre* (doctrine of the two realms) was critically introduced by the Reformed theologian Karl Barth. Barth claimed that the distinction between God's realm (or Christ's) and the worldly realm resulted in (or even aimed at) the church's withdrawal from the world. By ascribing autonomy to the worldly spheres of politics, economy or culture, the Lutheran tradition, in Barth's view, diminished the "reign of Christ" (*Königsherrschaft Christi*), which extended to the whole cosmos. Thus, it participated in the ideas of modernity, which Barth interpreted as a process of emancipation from God.

I find Barth's critique of modernity one-sided. In any case, the distinction between the two realms was not meant to qualify God's caring attitude toward the world. Although the term realm might suggest a spatial separation of two different spaces that are situated side by side and have nothing in common, the alternative terminology of the two regiments (*zwei Regimente*) shows that the distinction identifies two different ways in which God governs God's one world, or the two different ways in which God cares for God's one world: on the one hand by revealing and spreading God's *euangelion*; on the other, by establishing a stable order that warrants peace in social life. Luther calls the first one God's "proper work" (*opus proprium*) because spreading the gospel purely expresses God's very essence, which is love. The second one is God's "extrinsic work" (*opus alienum*) because it is only necessary for external reasons, namely human sin that causes disorder and destruction in society. It is the political authority's God-given duty then to fight disorder and to establish, organize and safeguard a stable and peaceful order of human beings' external life. Of course this is also motivated by God's love because it is part of God's *conservatio mundi*: God does not leave us alone with the mess that we have created ourselves. But it is not a direct expression of God's love, for the authorities must have the competence and ability to oblige people to obey the rules or to use force in order to overcome violence. This does not always look like an act of love.

The distinction between the two realms has a number of consequences, both for the church and the world. For the church this implies a critique of any attempt to foster the spreading of the gospel by means of external coercion. The famous words of CA XXVIII, namely that the bishops should preach the gospel *sine vi humana, sed verbo*, "without human force, but rather through God's word alone," exactly describe the character of the church's *opus proprium*: convincing, not coercing. The Reformers trusted in the convincing power of God's word itself. We may wonder why this did not immediately lead to the idea of religious freedom and tolerance and may recall the acts of intolerance and religious coercion that the Reformers were able and willing to perform: the expulsion of Karlstadt, the persecution of the "Anabaptists," the uninhibited polemics against the Jews, to name but a few.

Seen from today's perspective, this is an obvious self-contradiction. However, I believe that in these cases the Reformers did not argue with the *opus proprium* but with the *opus alienum*. They thought that the propagation of alternative interpretations of the gospel (not to speak of heresies) would confuse the people and lead to controversial debates that could jeopardize peace in society. So they considered it to be a part of the state's responsibility to protect the citizens from this confusion. Unlike today, the peaceful coexistence of people of different religious backgrounds seemed impossible in the sixteenth century. Moreover, the legal system, too, had not yet been truly disconnected from religion and therefore heresy, such as contesting the doctrine of the Trinity or the baptism of children, constituted a crime that had to be prosecuted. The *sine vi humana sed verbo* unfolded its full potential only centuries after the Reformation.

As to the world, it is crucial to recognize that the Reformers distinguished between the two realms: they did not regard the *civitas terrena* as *civitas Diaboli*. Of course, Luther in particular, reckoned with the power of the devil. In his famous hymn, "A Mighty Fortress is our God," he even called him "this world's prince," adding that "on earth is not his equal." This, however, does not mean that the world is a sphere beyond God's power that Christians have to flee. The Lutheran Reformation did not support escapism or "quietism" as has often been argued. On the contrary, this world continues to be governed by God, and God limits the devil's power by making rules and creating institutions to safeguard the good order of the social world. Therefore Christians are entitled and even obliged to participate in the duty of maintaining the social order. This is clearly expressed in CA XVI,

> Concerning civic affairs they teach that lawful civil ordinances are good works of God and that Christians are permitted to hold civil office, to work in law courts, to decide matters by imperial and other existing laws, to impose just punishments, to wage just war, to serve as soldiers, to make legal contracts, to hold property, to take an oath when required by magistrates, to take a wife, to be given in marriage.[6]

The Confession explicitly condemns first "the Anabaptists who prohibit Christians from assuming such civil offices,"[7] and second "those who locate

---

[6] "The Augsburg Confession—Latin Text—Article XVI: Civic Affairs," in Robert Kolb and Timothy J. Wengert (eds), *The Book of Concord* (Minneapolis: Fortress Press, 2000), 49. The Augsburg Confession's condemnation of the Anabaptists had been used by some Reformers to justify the persecution of Anabaptists. At its Eleventh Assembly in 2010, the LWF asked Mennonites for forgiveness and committed to interpret the Lutheran Confessions in light of the "jointly described history between Lutherans and Anabaptists." See *Healing Memories. Implications of the Reconciliation between Lutherans and Mennonites*, LWF Studies 2016/4 (Geneva: The Lutheran World Federation, 2016), 132.
[7] *BC*, 49.

evangelical perfection not in the fear of God and in faith but in abandoning civil responsibilities"[8] (addressed to the claim that monastic life constitutes the perfect form of Christian life). Repeatedly, the Confession insists that the gospel aims at "justice of the heart" and does not demand an alternative lifestyle that competes with (and retreats from) the "civil ordinances" such as state or family.

The Confession almost inconspicuously hints at the Reformers' theological assessment of civic life. It is condensed in the word "love".." The gospel itself—as the Confession puts it—"requires [...] the exercise of love in these ordinances."[9] "Civic affairs," in other words, are the place where (and not beyond which) Christians are to exercise love of the neighbor. To engage in civic affairs, thus, is a matter of Christian love. This does not only mean that Christians are requested to practice love also when dealing with civic affairs. Rather, it implies that civic affairs are institutions of love themselves because God established them to give social life a stable order that frames and structures people's peaceful life. This is why Lutherans have always emphasized loyalty to the state's authority and institutions. It is well known that this has been criticized as "Lutheran authoritarianism," which has led Lutherans to long-term heteronomy. As a result, Lutheran churches were dependent on the state and prevented from developing or fostering a culture of civil society. Historically, we must admit that there is some truth to this, particularly in Germany. From a more systematic perspective I see considerable potential in the idea that human well-being requires stable institutions (or institutions of stability) and that loyalty to these institutions, taking responsibility for their maintenance and further development, is an expression of Christian love.

This idea has, of course, to be adapted to the structures and standards of modern society. When the Augsburg Confession states that "Consequently, Christians owe obedience to their magistrates and laws" (CA XVI),[10] we need to consider what this implies today in light of the structures of modern societies which, according to the sociologist Niklas Luhmann,[11] are no longer hierarchical and mono-centered but "functionally differentiated," and in which the political system is much more participatory than it was in the sixteenth century. Obeying the magistrates may rather mean being loyal to the procedures of democratic decision making, accepting the results of elections, being willing to stand for office, etc. The Confession also mentions the law. Obeying the law today might include defending the right to

---

[8] Ibid.
[9] Ibid.
[10] Ibid., 51
[11] Cf. Niklas Luhmann, *Soziale Systeme* (Frankfurt a.M.: Suhrkamp, 1984).

have rights, namely the civil or human rights that are incorporated into many constitutions, fighting corruption and other illegal forms of taking advantage, etc.

It is essential to see that the Confession does not demand unconditional "obedience to their magistrates and laws." Repeatedly, it speaks of "just punishment" or "just wars" and of "lawful civil ordinances," and thus, by implementing the category of justice, indicates that not every law and magistrate may be regarded as the "good works of God." Explicitly, moreover, after the phrase "Christians owe obedience to their magistrates and laws," it adds, "except when commanded to sin. For then they owe greater obedience to God than to human beings (Acts 5 [:29])."[12]

Luther was very hesitant with this restriction. To him, the order in itself was such a blessing that he was willing to prefer a bad order to the chaos that protests and rebellions were likely to cause. In case of necessary resistance, he therefore preferred passive martyrdom to active opposition. But this has remained a matter of debate within the Lutheran tradition. In any case, qualifying obedience indicates an "anti-totalitarian impulse" that fits very well with the distinction between the "two realms": The "realm of the world" is not the sphere of perfection and absolute decisions, but the sphere of imperfection and preferences. In his papers on "Ethics,"[13] Dietrich Bonhoeffer appropriately introduced the category of the "penultimate" to characterize the questions of worldly life, the sphere of ethical decisions. These "penultimate" questions do not determine the "ultimate" question of eternal salvation but have their own dignity, precisely because of that. For the Christian faith, they are neither a field of indifference (anything goes) nor a space of permanent *status confessionis*. Worldly life is supposed to witness, express and reflect the faith of the "heart" through the "bodily" works of love. The sphere of "works" very seldom requires an exclusive "either/or." Mostly it is a sphere of "more or less," that means, it implies a spectrum of possibilities that are "more or less" appropriate expressions of Christian love. It cannot be decided in advance what is more and what is less. It depends on the context, which might also change. This idea is fundamental to Paul's ethic: "everything is lawful, but not everything builds up," and "test everything; hold fast to what is good."[14]

---

[12] *BC*, 51.

[13] Cf. Dietrich Bonhoeffer, *Works*, vol. 6, Ethics, ed. Clifford J. Green, transl. Reinhard Krauss et al. (Minneapolis: Fortress Press, 2005).

[14] Cf. Bernd Oberdorfer, "A New Life in Christ: Pauline Ethics, and its Lutheran Reception," in Eve-Marie Becker and Kenneth Mtata (eds), *Pauline Hermeneutics: Exploring the "Power of the Gospel,"* LWF Studies 2016/3 (Leipzig: Evangelische Verlagsanstalt, 2016), 159; 163.

What follows from this in terms of the impact of theology on social life? I will conclude with some brief remarks referring to one famous, highly controversial example of how Luther dealt with questions of social ethics: his notorious statements during the Peasants' War.

Luther on the Peasants' War: Concluding remarks

Given that today the church is frequently advised to remain silent *in rebus politicis* because this is supposedly not its business, it is remarkable in itself that Luther commented on politics. Of course, he was a public figure, whose every statement was collected (cf. the *Tischreden*) and disseminated. Yet, he did not simply present his opinions as a "public intellectual" (as we would put it today), but deliberately as a theologian. Consistently with his concept of the "two realms," he did not claim the role of ultimate referee in matters of culture, politics or economy. He emphasized that the church has no superior knowledge in these spheres. And he also made clear that the Bible does not offer concrete prescriptions for how to build a house, govern a state, educate children, run a business, etc. Nevertheless, he did not hesitate to speak out on social conflicts and political crises. Of particular significance are his public statements during the Peasants' War of 1525.[15]

Luther felt impelled to comment for several reasons. First, the peasants relied on his reformatory idea of "Christian freedom" when demanding freedom from their lords. Thus, these lords could accuse him of being responsible for the riots. Second, the peasants derived their political and economic demands directly from the gospel. Third, they fought for their issue in a non-legal, violent way, disobeying the authorities and destabilizing the order of society. Therefore, although he regarded the peasants' complaints about being treated unjustly by their lords as legitimate on the whole and supported many of their political demands, he believed that the peasants were wrong in at least two respects. They confused law and gospel by making the gospel law, and they disdained the rules and principles that are valid in God's worldly realm by violently rebelling against the authorities and changing order into chaos. So, on the one hand he criticized the nobility for treating the peasants badly and strongly requested them to comply with the peasants' legitimate demands, while, on the other, he emphatically challenged them to stave off the rebellion with the harshest

---

[15] Cf. esp. Martin Luther, "Admonition to Peace referring to the Twelve Articles of the Peasants' Union in Swabia," in *WA* 18, 291–334, *LW* 46, 3–43; "Against the Murderous, Thieving Hordes of Peasants," in *WA* 18, 357–61, *LW* 46, 45–55; "Open Letter on the Harsh Book Against the Peasants," in *WA* 18, 384–401, *LW* 46, 57–85.

possible means. He even reminded them that they did God's work when using their swords against the rebelling peasants. In other words, he urged them to use force in the name of God.

We might tend to say, *si tacuisses*—if [only] you had remained silent. But even in these notorious, horrible, rude and almost blasphemous words we can still discover the Reformer's positive assessment of the world as a sphere of God's caring and conserving power. Luther's concern was to protect and to stabilize the social order essential for a peaceful life. He was convinced that in a world contaminated by sin it is sometimes necessary to use force. Yet, in contrast to his aggressive verbal outburst against the peasants, he strictly bound the use of force to the law and legitimacy. Some years later, in his 1532 series of sermons on the Sermon on the Mount, he explicitly stated that princes who start a war without a legitimate reason should be called "children of the devil" rather than "children of God," and he requested people who suffered injustice to go to court instead of taking revenge individually.[16] In principle, this is consistent with his statements on the Peasants' War. He criticized the peasants for not following the path of the law when pursuing their concerns, and exclusively addressed the state authority to end the rebellion with force. However, by legitimizing unlimited force, he damaged his cause, and for centuries Lutherans have been confronted with the image of being devoted servants to the state, unable to raise a critical voice and to put limits to the authority of the state. It took centuries until Lutherans clearly recognized that the concept of the "two realms" allowed them to support the emergence of a civil society that would resist totalitarian excesses of the state.

This example might warn us to be cautious in our political statements; they are not straight from heaven. They are always at risk of eventually being proven to be false. They have to be continuously reevaluated in light of the principles of Lutheran social ethics. These principles not only allow for but even require an active involvement of Lutherans and the Lutheran churches in the processes of developing a society, "in which justice dwells." The concept of the "two realms" does not prevent but rather encourages this involvement, precisely because we cannot save the world, we can merely engage with it.

---

[16] Cf. Bernd Oberdorfer, "How Do We Deal with a Challenging Text," in Kenneth Mtata and Craig Koester (eds), *To All the Nations. Lutheran Hermeneutics and the Gospel of Matthew*, LWF Studies 2015/2 (Leipzig: Evangelische Verlagsanstalt, 2015), 75–88.

Just Peacemaking: Christian Pacifism as a Form of Political Responsibility

John D. Roth

Introduction

In the following essay I reflect on Christian pacifism as a form of political responsibility from the perspective of the Mennonite (or Anabaptist) tradition.

Theology is always embedded in larger political and economic contexts. The Reformation world of the sixteenth century, like today, was fraught with profound economic disparities and deep political tensions, in which violence was never far from the surface. In the fall of 1524, the economic frustrations of Germany's peasants and artisans spilled over into widespread revolution—the Peasants' War of 1525. At the same time, the threat of an advancing Turkish army—accompanied by deep fears of Islam—was on the minds of all Europeans. In 1521, Suleiman the Magnificent had conquered most of Hungary; by 1529, his armies had laid siege to Vienna—the last major defense of Europe to the east.

In the midst of this political, economic and social turmoil, European Christians were asking themselves basic questions about the gospel, and particularly questions about the teachings of Jesus. What counsel did Christ have to offer in the face of political and economic upheaval? At several key moments, Luther acknowledged these questions and responded with decisive clarity. In the spring of 1525, for example, he called on the European nobility to crush the peasants' revolt as an expression of their Christian duty.[1] The following year he wrote the treatise, "Whether Soliders, Too,

---

[1] Martin Luther, "Against the Robbing and Murdering Hordes of Peasants, 1525," in *LW* 46, 50 ff. "Whoever is the first to put [a seditious person] to death does right and well," [...] Therefore let everyone who can, smite, slay, and stab, secretly or openly, remember that nothing can be more poisonous, hurtful, or devilish than a rebel."

Can be Saved?" thus fulfilling a promise he had made to an officer, whose conscience was troubled by the bloodshed and carnage of the Peasants' War. There Luther answered the question posed by the title in the affirmative.[2] It would be best, of course, if all Christians were to follow the teachings of Christ to love everyone, including their enemies; and clearly, no Christian could use violence for private gain. But if the appropriate authorities should seek help in maintaining public order or defending against an outside attack, Christians should have no hesitation to serve as soldiers. Luther repeated this argument three years later in his treatise "On War Against the Turk." Responsibility for warfare against the Turk rested ultimately with the emperor; but if the emperor called on Christians to fight, they should do so without reservation.[3]

At their core, none of these arguments were new—they were simply a reframing of the long-standing Just War tradition, carried forward today among modern Christians in the formulation of "Responsibility to Protect," or R2P.[4]

At the same time that Luther was responding to the crisis of rebellious peasants and Turkish aggression, an alternative perspective emerged among a small group of Christians who would become known as the Anabaptists. The Anabaptists borrowed heavily from Luther's principle of *sola scriptura*, his critique of the papacy, as well as his insights regarding the "priesthood of all believers." But they broke with the Reformers—and the deeper Catholic tradition—in their understanding of political responsibility. Rejecting the Just War tradition, the Anabaptists argued that following Christ was incompatible with lethal violence—that Christians were called to love their enemies, even though it offered no guarantee of immediate political outcome and might result in the death of innocent people.

This brief essay offers a short summary of the Anabaptist understanding of the gospel of peace—a conviction that is perhaps as fundamental to the Anabaptist understanding of Christian faithfulness as the doctrine of grace has been for Lutherans. Following that summary, I want to suggest several ways that this commitment has found expression in daily life—a brief description of an Anabaptist-Mennonite "political theology"—and the essay will close with a few stories from the global church today.

---

[2] Martin Luther, "Whether Soldiers, Too, Can Be Saved, 1526," in *LW* 46, 93–137; *WA* 19:623–662.

[3] Martin Luther, "On War Against the Turk, 1529," in *LW* 46, 161–205; *WA* 30/2:107–48.

[4] Cf. Alex J. Bellamy, "The Responsibility to Protect and the Just War Tradition," in Ramesh Thakur and William Maley (eds), *Theorizing the Responsibility to Protect* (Cambridge: Cambridge University Press, 2015), 181–99.

ANABAPTIST UNDERSTANDINGS OF THE GOSPEL OF PEACE

The Anabaptists—and the Mennonite, Amish and Hutterite groups who descended from them—rejected infant baptism in part because they believed that faith could not be coerced. They were not Pelegianists, committed to a doctrine of works-righteousness but they were convinced that following Jesus required a conscious decision to accept God's gracious gift of forgiveness—something no infant could do.[5]

At stake in this commitment were fundamental questions of loyalty, identity and allegiance. Baptism not only marked the believer's spiritual transformation before God, but it also signaled formal membership into a body of believers whose identity was distinct from the general society.

Furthermore, baptism was about *metanoia*—repentance; turning around—that was expressed in a transformed life of daily discipleship (*Nachfolge Christi*). Through the Holy Spirit, Jesus' followers participated in a "new creation"—a new form of politics that had tangible social, economic and political consequences. Thus, for example, the Anabaptists assumed that following Jesus would change the way in which Christians regarded their possessions. Some groups, like the Hutterites, shared all possessions in common. Others practiced radical mutual aid, with the understanding that each member would share freely as the need arose. The Anabaptists also took seriously Christ's admonition to refrain from swearing oaths, arguing that Christians should always speak the truth and honor commitments.

But perhaps the most problematic ethical teaching of the Anabaptists was their renunciation of lethal force. Already in the fall of 1524, as tensions among the peasants escalated, Conrad Grebel, a leader among the dissenters in Zurich, challenged Thomas Müntzer to reject the sword: "The gospel and its adherents," Grebel wrote, "are not to be protected by the sword, nor [should] they [protect] themselves. [...] True believing Christians are sheep among wolves, sheep for the slaughter. [...] They use neither worldly sword nor war, since killing has ceased with them entirely."[6]

---

[5] There are many summaries of the early Anabaptist movement. For Lutheran lay readers, a useful point of departure is a jointly written account ("Telling the Sixteenth-Century Story Together") that comprised a significant part of the final report of the Lutheran-Mennonite International Study Commission published as *Healing Memories: Reconciling in Christ: Report of the Lutheran-Mennonite International Study Commission* (Leipzig: Evangelische Verlagsanstalt, 2010), 20-72, at https://www.lutheranworld.org/sites/default/files/dtpw-studies-201602-healing_memories-en-full.pdf

[6] Leland Harder (ed.), *The Sources of Swiss Anabaptism: The Grebel Letters and Related Documents* (Scottdale, PA: Herald Press, 1985), 290.

It may be tempting to regard this as an unsophisticated and naïve instance of biblical literalism. Yet, the Anabaptist perspective on pacifism—what became known as the "gospel of peace"—is actually rooted in a much deeper political theology. The outlines of that argument go something like this.

In the opening chapters of the book of Genesis we find a description of what God had in mind when God created the world and human beings. In Genesis 1 and 2 God made man and woman with the intention that they would live in harmony—in Shalom—with each other, with God and with the natural world. In our deepest design, humans were intended by God to live in wholeness, intimacy, trust and vulnerability with each other and with God. This is the purpose for which we were made; this is our *original* design.

Yet, as we know, the world that we live in does not look like this. Sin and pride are also part of the Genesis story. As a consequence of sin, Adam and Eve hide from God; they are alienated from each other; and they find themselves at war with nature. Already in the first generation, Cain kills Abel in a fit of jealousy; and human history since then has been a record dripping with the blood of human violence—of family feuds, of civil wars, of slavery and tyranny, wars of oppression and wars of liberation. So that history can easily be read as a ceaseless quest for power—as the "law of the jungle" thinly disguised with the veneer of civilization.

But the biblical story makes clear that this is not the full picture. In the Bible we also find an account of God patiently and persistently calling human beings back to Godself, inviting them to live as they were intended: in peace, intimacy, vulnerability, trust. The Bible is the story of God's invitation—not coerced, but an invitation—for human beings to recover their true identity and to live in a deeper reality of Shalom that has been distorted by sin and violence.

How do we recover our true selves? One answer in the Hebrew Scriptures is by trusting in God rather than in human power. Thus, Abram leaves the comfort of Ur, trusting in God's promise. Moses and the children of Israel trust God to provide as they wander in the desert. Even during the wars of conquest, the children of Israel were admonished to "trust in God rather than the strength of kings, or armies, or chariots of iron." "God is our refuge and strength," writes the Psalmist, "a very present help in trouble" (Ps 46:1).

But Christians have also read the Hebrew Scriptures as a story pointing forward to the fullness of God's revelation—to the coming of a Messiah who will restore humanity to the wholeness which God intended, to the healing of a broken creation. Christians understand this Messiah—Jesus—to be the fullest expression of God's character. In Jesus, the will of God is made incarnate. Thus, God's revelation in Christ is not simply a nice set of enlightened ethical teachings. Rather, it is a fundamentally new way of seeing reality.

For one thing, Jesus calls his followers to rethink all the assumptions about status, power, security and success that once seemed obvious. "You have heard that it was said ..." Jesus told his listeners in the Sermon on the Mount, "You shall love your neighbor and hate your enemy." That is the teaching of the law; that is justice; that is the logic of common sense. "But I say unto you, Love your enemies and pray for those who persecute you..." (Mt 5:43–44). Or, "You have heard that it was said, 'An eye for an eye and a tooth for a tooth' "—it makes sense; that's only fair. "But I say to you, Do not resist an evildoer. But if anyone strikes you on the right cheek, turn the other also" (Mt 5:38–39).

The same theme is echoed also in other passages; it is not the wealthy or the powerful or the strong who are blessed by God, but rather the poor in spirit, the meek, the pure in heart, those who are merciful (Mt 5:3–9). In this new way of life, "the last will be first, and the first will be last" (Mt 20:16). To enter this kingdom you need to become like a child (Mt 18:3). If you want to be great, be a servant (Mk 10:43); if you want to save your life, be ready to lose it (Lk 9:24).

When his followers hailed him as a liberator from Roman oppression, he greeted them atop a donkey, not a war horse. In his final opportunity to instruct his disciples, Jesus washed their dirty feet. And, in the face of false accusations and a sham trial, Jesus allowed himself to be killed rather than to call on the armies of angels at his disposal.

Yet, as we know, the cross was not the end of the story. In fact, for Christians this is the beginning of the story, because in the resurrection that followed, God made it clear that death and violence do not have the final word. Our fear that death is the worst thing that can happen to us turns out to be a part of the fallen world. In the resurrection Christians proclaim that life and love are more powerful than violence and death.

To be sure, all of this transcends ordinary human logic. It would make much more "sense" to argue that we should defend our interests and those of our neighbors; that we should draw a sharp line between Good and Evil; that we should seek retribution for evildoers. Yet, as Jesus taught, there is no particular virtue in loving those who love you. Indeed, the basic principles of the Just War theory are actually rooted in the writings of Cicero, who lived two centuries before Christ. Just War arguments remind us of principles like "fairness" and "justice," which are not bad things in and of themselves. But it is not clear that they point to the Christian gospel.

Indeed, in the USA, Christians are the group most likely to support the nation's wars as well as the government's use of torture.[7] One might find this

---

[7] See, for example, David Neff, "Evangelicals and Torture: A new study says white evangelicals are most likely to justify torture. What should we make of that?," in *Gleanings* (1 May 2009), at http://www.christianitytoday.com/gleanings/2009/may/evangelicals-and-torture.html .

outrageous, but for a great deal of church history this has been the "political responsibility" of Christianity: claiming God as a tribal deity who can be called on to defend political order—so that the church serves as a chaplain to the self-interest of the nation state: blessing its wars, providing spiritual relief to troubled consciences; giving divine sanction to its authority. Today the cemeteries of Europe and parts of Africa are filled with gravestones of Christians who died killing other Christians—each convinced that they were fighting a "Just War," honoring God by killing—for their country or tribe.

The gospel of peace reminds Christians that Jesus is Lord of the whole world; that their allegiance to the body of Christ comes before allegiance to the nation or tribe. It calls Christians to take seriously the claim that in Christ, "There is no longer Jew or Greek, there is no longer slave or free, there is no longer male and female; for all of you are one …" (Gal 3:28).

JUST PEACEMAKING

But in what sense are Christian pacifists "politically responsible"?[8] Isn't all of this really an argument for sectarian withdrawal—a retreat into some form of moral purity that looks on passively while innocent people suffer at the hands of bullies and thugs?

In response to these concerns, let me begin with several confessions. I recognize that even as a pacifist I cannot escape my complicity in the systems and structures of coercion: I pay taxes, some of which support the military. I live in a community whose laws are enforced by the local police. I carry a passport issued by a country that defends its borders with an army. Pacifist Christians do not stand on some sort of high ground of absolute "moral purity."

But we still have meaningful choices: and one clear choice is a commitment not to take the life of another human being who is made in the image of God or to encourage others to do so in my name.

So what does "political responsibility" look like for the Christian pacifist?

- First, Christian pacifists are active in the daily life of civil society: nurturing healthy relationships within their families; participating in the complex web of human interaction in schools, churches and

---

[8] Portions of what follows draw on an essay previously published as John D. Roth, "Pacifism as Political Responsibility? The Position of the Dissenters in the 16th Century," in Irene Dingel and Christiane Tietz (eds), *Die politische Aufgabe von Religion: Perspektiven der drei monotheistischen Religionen* (Göttingen: Vandenhoek & Ruprecht, 2011), 331–44.

voluntary associations; obeying the law in every way that does not conflict with their commitment to Christ; respecting and praying for people in positions of political authority.

- Second, Christian pacifists also serve the common good by standing alongside people on the margins, speaking out on behalf of the poor, the refugees, the dispossessed and those without a voice, assuring them that they have not been forgotten. In my community, a disproportionate number of Christian pacifists are active in homeless shelters, after-school programs, adult literacy initiatives and especially in health care projects that reach out to the most vulnerable members of our communities. The experience of conscientious objectors serving in mental health hospitals in the USA during World War II has led to fundamental reforms in how the nation treats people with mental disabilities.

- Third, Christian pacifists have been especially active in various forms of conflict resolution, especially at the grassroots levels. The Victim-Offender Reconciliation Program—a community-based initiative started by pacifist Christians—has been enthusiastically supported by courts throughout the US and now has local chapters in hundreds of communities and in twelve countries. Other conflict transformation programs are finding support in many settings around the world. In contrast to the seductively quick solutions that violence offers, peace building is a long process, requiring a deep understanding of culture, an appreciation for the complexities of human nature, a recognition that relationships must be built on trust and, ultimately, a capacity for patience. Christian pacifists recognize that we may not see the fruits of our labors within the standard election cycles, or even within our lifetime.

- Fourth, some Christian pacifists have helped to challenge oppressive and violent regimes through nonviolent direct action: I would never argue that pacifism will always "work" as a political strategy—this position should not be confused with the optimism of secular liberals who insist that pacifist solutions will guarantee political "success." But I do not think that we have fully grasped the significance of the church's role in the collective protests that have brought an end to dictatorships in the Philippines, Poland, East Germany, South Africa and elsewhere. "As soon as they started shooting us," Lech Welesa said of the nonviolent solidarity movement in Poland, "I knew that we had won."

- Finally, Christian pacifists serve the common good in public expressions of lament and hope. Any time human beings die violent deaths—

under any circumstances—Christians should publicly lament. Public lament serves as a reminder that violence is always an aberration, an unwelcome intrusion into the world as it should be. On the other side of lament is the hope for an alternative future, the hope expressed by millions of Christians every day when they pray: "thy kingdom come, God … thy will be done; on earth as it is in heaven."

In all these, and many other forms of witness, Christian pacifists exercise their "political responsibilities," by engaging in these activities not primarily as citizens, or as a political party, or as a lobby group shouting to be heard, but as members of the body of Christ, as ambassadors of the Prince of Peace who came as a servant, who welcomed children and foreigners into his circle, and who taught us to love our enemies.

SAYING NO!

I suspect that up until this point most readers would agree with the general direction of my reflections. These forms of peacemaking would be shared by virtually all Christians—indeed, all people of good will.

But for the Christian pacifist, the "yes" to just peacemaking is also accompanied by a clear "no." And here is where the conversation becomes more difficult. Just War arguments, even in their refurbished expression of "Responsibility to Protect," ultimately seek to provide Christians with a narrative that can justify their participation in lethal violence; that is a step that Christian pacifists refuse to take. The refusal to cross that line should not be confused with a retreat into sectarian purity … or a denial of the reality of evil in the world.

Rather, it is a radical form of witness, rooted in an eschatological view of history that rejects the argument that Christians must participate in evil so that history will "come out right." In the resurrection, God has already prevailed over death; and at the end of time God will prevail over the forces of evil. The Lamb has conquered. This is the truth to which Christians are called to witness, even if that witness comes in the form of martyrdom.

CONCLUSION

Let me conclude with two brief stories.

On 26 December 2004, a 9.2 magnitude earthquake—with its epicenter just off the west coast of Sumatra, Indonesia—unleashed a deadly tsunami in the Indian Ocean. Within hours, the force of the tsunami struck the coastal town of Aceh, killing 170,000 inhabitants and leaving more than 500,000 people without food or housing. Among the many relief workers who arrived quickly in the aftermath of the crisis was an unlikely team of Mennonites and Muslims from the Indonesian town of Solo.

For decades, Solo had been a center of various conservative militant Muslim groups, including several who had explicitly advocated the use of violence to achieve their aims. Relations in Solo between Muslims and Christians—including a small group of Indonesian Mennonites—were filled with tension, sometimes breaking out into bloody conflict.

In 2004, Paulus Hartono, a Javanese Mennonite pastor in Solo initiated contact with the leader of the Hizbullah militia group, offering to help mediate a dispute over the group's radio station. Initially, the Hizbullah commander brusquely turned him away. Yet Hartono refused to give up. As a cofounder of the Forum for Peace across Religions and Groups, Hartono was determined to put his convictions into action. So he continued to stop by the Hizbullah offices for tea and conversation. Eventually, the commander allowed Hartono to mediate the conflict, and the two men slowly became friends.

When the tsunami struck Aceh several months later, Hartono made a bold proposal. He invited the commander and members of the Hizbullah group to join in a relief effort, led by the Mennonites of Solo and funded in part by Mennonite Central Committee. Throughout 2005, Indonesian Mennonites and conservative Muslims worked alongside each other helping to restore destroyed homes and to repair damaged churches and mosques.

In the years since then, the Hizbullah commander has asked Hartono's peace organization to lead conflict transformation workshops for his group, including several seminars at the Center for the Study and Promotion of Peace in Duta Wacana Christian University. His hope, the commander explained, was that participants would come to think of themselves as "agents of peace." One Muslim volunteer reported to Hartono, "Thank you for this disaster response program. We know now that the Christian church and people are not as we thought before."[9]

At the same time, however, I need to tell another story that continues to unfold in our family of faith. Most readers will be familiar with the story of the abduction of some 275 girls from a Christian school in Chibok, Nigeria, in April 2014. One hundred seventy-three of those girls were members of the Ekklesiyar Yan'uwa a Nigeria (EYN), an Anabaptist-related church of some 500,000 members in northeastern Nigeria, precisely the territory most affected by Boko Haram. Since then, some 1700 EYN churches have

---

[9] Jeanne Jantzi and Tim Shenk, "Indonesian Mennonites and Muslims Work Together after Earthquake," in *A Common Place* (October 2010), 4-6.

been destroyed, church headquarters overrun, 11,000 members killed and another 80,000 forced to flee their homes. Some ten to fifteen years ago, before Boko Haram entered the picture, the EYN church recommitted itself to the gospel of peace. For more than a decade they have pondered Jesus's teachings in the Sermon on the Mount and they have included prayers in their weekly worship service explicitly for their enemies. And now their faith has been tested … over and over.

"Please pray for us," one leader said recently. "We are finding strength in the Word of God. The Word of God revealed in Jesus Christ is the truth we preach. Yes, we are tempted to retaliate. But the Word of God has given us direction—don't hit back. You are more in charge when you let go than when you take control."[10]

That may sound like a weak response to Islamic radicalism. But it is not all that they have been doing. Alongside the urgent work of caring for refugees and comforting bereaved families, the EYN has also committed itself to collecting the names and the stories of every single person who has died. The infamous Soviet leader Joseph Stalin once said that "the death of one person is a tragedy; the death of a millions is a statistic." When we hear of 11,000 people killed in Nigeria, it is easy for our minds to go numb with the sheer enormity of that number. Yet every single one of those people was a mother, a father, a son, a daughter, a friend—a Christian believer—whose life matters. By gathering the names and the stories of their martyrs, by holding them up in public memory, the EYN church is planting the seeds of a profound Christian witness for coming generations. Every life matters to God; each life matters to the church—their deaths will not go forgotten or ignored.

I conclude by inviting you to consider two scenarios. The first scenario is our current reality—a world of deep, pervasive violence that jars our senses every time we read a newspaper or watch the evening news. I live in a culture that is dominated by fear: since 2001, my country has created a Department of Homeland Security; we have occupied two countries; we have spent more than USD 3 trillion in the war on terror; we have curtailed immigration and have restricted the liberties of citizens. Yet, even in the most wealthy and powerful nation on earth, we still live in fear.

Abroad, our world is dominated night after night with reports of more suicide bombings; more homes bulldozed in Palestine; more refugees displaced; more children orphaned. Ours is a world where violence begets

---

[10] "Address to the Annual Conference by EYN President Rev. Dr Samuel Dante Dali," in *Church of the Brethren Newsline* (13 July 2015), at http://www.brethren.org/news/2015/ac/eyn-president-address-to-annual-conference.html?referrer=https://www.google.com/.

violence—with each side certain that it is fighting a Just War; that its cause is on the side of the righteous and the good.

In the midst of all this, Christians are invited to bear witness to a different sort of reality. In the midst of the violence around us, the Gospel of Peace offers a candle of hope. The God we serve invites rather than compels. The Jesus we claim as Lord came to earth in the form of a servant; taught his followers to love their enemies; and allowed himself to be killed rather than to defend the truth with violence. His triumph was an assertion of the power of life over the power of death.

The truth of Christian pacifism is a vulnerable truth, offered as an invitation, not an argument. The flicker of that candle might seem tiny and insignificant; it may not illuminate all the corners where darkness holds sway. The gospel of peace offers no promise of political success; there are no guarantees that non-violent love will convince every tyrant to put down their weapon. But by holding up the light, Christians bear witness to the world that the darkness of violence will not prevail; that love is stronger than fear; that life in Christ is more powerful than the threat of death; that allegiance to the body of Christ comes before our allegiance to the nation state; and that history is ultimately shaped not by human might nor by power but by the spirit of the living God.

For pacifist Christians in the tradition of the sixteenth-century dissenters, this is what it means to be "politically responsible."

Confessing the Past: Attempts in the Evangelical Lutheran Church in Hungary to Evaluate its Role during the Cold War

Tamás Fabiny

"That need which must confess the past"

In 2005, the synod of the Evangelical Lutheran Church in Hungary created a committee, including an historian, an archivist, a lawyer and a theologian, to look into the church's past. It was tasked with carrying out detailed research into church life between 1945 and 1990, specifically focusing on certain persons' cooperation with the state security services. At the time, Hungary was under Soviet occupation and the state—officially called a proletarian dictatorship—expressly aimed at oppressing the churches.

The committee officially looked into different documents (from the somewhat incomplete archives) and started to produce publications, which include original sources that shed light onto the collaboration of certain members of the church leadership. The committee initially examined the past of the present church leadership. The people mentioned in the documents are given the opportunity to make personal statements but, at the same time, the results of the research are published with the actual names.

I shall take as a starting point a quotation from a frequently cited Hungarian poet, Attila József, who stated "that need which must confess the past."[1] Not only Hungary, but the whole region, is struggling with the heritage of

---

[1] Attila József, *Poems*, ed. by Thomas Kabdebo and transl. by Vernon Watkins (London: The Danubia Book Co., 1966).

the recent past and trying to take steps toward an authentic and therapeutic recognition of the past. This is not easy. The systematic research carried out on secret service documents in Germany is well known. The so-called *Gauck-Behörde* (named after a former pastor from East Germany, president of Germany from March 2012 to March 2017) was an unquestionable authority. Based on its work, the role East Germany and the churches played during the Communist era was processed already quite early on—of course not without controversy. In Hungary, systematic and scientifically-based research of the past was not initiated immediately after the regime change. Therefore, sensitive stories became fertile terrain for the yellow press on the one hand and political blackmail on the other. Not many chose to face their own or their family's past openly and voluntarily. There where it did happen, we witnessed personal tragedies. One of the greatest contemporary Hungarian writers, Péter Esterházy, published the book *Harmonia caelestis* (2000), which is in part a tribute to his father. Later the author learned that his father, who was of aristocratic origin, had been greatly humiliated during the Communist regime and had submitted regular reports to the state security services between 1957 and 1980. In 2002, Esterházy published a book *Javított kiadás* (corrected version), which expresses his personal pain.

While we had hoped for balanced and well analyzed research of the past, suddenly lists of dubious origin appeared, showing that allegedly several church leaders had collaborated with the Communist state security services. Certain reports referred to lurking pastors and collaborating bishops and curators happily cooperating with the authorities. Churches were a success story for the state security services one could read in media headlines. Even more distasteful was the fact that in many stories pastors were accused of reporting on their own flock, and even violating the confidentiality of confession. It is unfair that the names of the (real or alleged) informers are made public while the names of the liaising officers or those receiving the reports have until today not been revealed. Furthermore, one must take into account that many documents were willingly destroyed or falsified.

What needs to be mentioned is the malicious activity of the State Office for Church Matters, a ministerial organization that was created for controlling and restricting church activity. Officially, an application had to be made to this authority for permission to be granted for any public church activity such as building operations; youth work; books and other publications. Today, we see that there were huge differences among pastors and bishops in whether they maintained merely an administrative connection to this office or used this contact for their own personal interest, sometimes harming other colleagues in the church.

In this paper, I will touch on the collaboration of bishops of the Evangelical Lutheran Church in Hungary with the Communist authorities, taking into account that officially they had to cooperate with the State Office for Church Matters. While church leaders were obliged to maintain these contacts in their position, it is striking that some bishops were employed as informers and many of them wrote reports to the state security services under code names.

The leadership of the Evangelical Lutheran Church in Hungary was the first church in Hungary and in our region—and also the only church leadership in Hungary—to acknowledge the need to research the past. In my inaugural speech as bishop in 2006, I thought it important to touch on the recognition of the past which, at the time, was quite a sensitive question. I spoke about working with our recent past in an honest, critical and therapeutic way.

> I have to speak about the unveiling of the recent past of our church history. I am deliberately raising this unresolved question here while listing our duties inside the church. I would not want the church to lag behind secular research, behind historians and the yellow press, as if it were constantly delaying the opening up of its past. This also applies to the so-called informers. In the last months, we have seen documents related to artists, sportsmen and women and politicians presented in manipulative ways. It is a warning for us that the church can choose another way. Not through blackmail and threatening, not with the intention to arouse sensation but in a brotherly and sisterly way, carrying each other's burdens, ready to apologize and forgive.[2]

While the secular media reacted quite positively to this program, the church members seemed to be more ambiguous. The research commenced in 2005 and the results are currently being published. The stories differ widely: there were persons who consciously harmed others or the whole church while many (sometimes out of fear or human weakness) cooperated with the state security services in a rather harmless way. It is quite clear that many of those who signed an agreement were not intending to cause harm to anybody and were motivated by the concern for the future of the church. Therefore, a profound analysis of the past, which does not stop at the identification of the persons behind the code names, is necessary.

At the time of church elections in 2012, the applicable church law[3] was modified, stipulating that for all positions from dean upwards the committee for the recognition of the past had to investigate whether the candidate used to collaborate with the state security services. From the very beginning, the members of the committee underlined that there were different ways of collaborating and different motivations for doing

---

[2] Inauguration speech of Bishop Dr Tamás Fabiny, 25 March 2006.
[3] Church law 2012/II. 6. § (1), effective as of 28 September 2012.

so and that therefore a personalized approach was needed. Furthermore, it is important not to forget the responsibility of those operating the state system and benefiting from it.

A CASE STUDY:
BISHOP ZOLTÁN KÁLDY AND BISHOP ERNŐ OTTLYK
AKA "PÉCSI" AND "LÁSZLÓ SZAMOSI"

As an example for collaboration with the hostile Communist state authorities, I would like to share some results of the research on the activity of two bishops, namely Ernő Ottlyk (1918–1995) and Zoltán Káldy (1919–1987). The latter was the President of the Lutheran World Federation (LWF) from 1984 until his death.

Káldy became bishop after the Communist regime had dismissed the lawful bishop, Lajos Ordass. Ordass was elected bishop in 1945, imprisoned in 1948 and practically kept under house arrest from 1950 to 1956. Just before the 1956 revolution, he was rehabilitated and resumed his service as bishop during the revolution. He was not only renowned in his own church but also internationally, and was elected Vice-President of the LWF at its first assembly in 1947 at Lund, and reelected in 1957, at its third assembly at Minneapolis. After the revolution had been staved off with the help of Soviet tanks, the Kádár government, backed by Moscow, started its repressions. In 1958 the bishop's seat was declared empty for administrative reasons and Ordass had to step back and the search for a new bishop started. Obviously one cannot speak of a free and fair election. Out of several politically strong candidates, pastor Zoltán Káldy, a popular pastor of the evangelization movement and dean of Pécs, was elected and installed in 1958 on the second anniversary of the suppression of the revolution. The state security services had already become active earlier during the seemingly democratic bishop's election procedure. A minister from the Ministry of Interior Affairs wrote in a memo of 16 July 1958, "We have operative goals with Zoltán Káldy as candidate for bishop."[4]

The documents show that the minister requested a meeting with Káldy, under the codename "Pécsi," at the end of September. He closes his report with the evaluation,

---

[4] Háló 2, *Dokumentumok és tanulmányok a Magyarországi Evangélikus Egyház és az állambiztonság kapcsolatáról 1945–1990. Egyházvezetők 1. Káldy Zoltán, Ottlyk Ernő* [Documents and Studies on the Relationship between the Evangelical Lutheran Church in Hungary and the State authorities between 1945–1990. Church leadership, part 1. Zoltán Káldy, Ernő Ottlyk] (Budapest: Luther Kiadó, 2014), 223.

At the meeting, "Pécsi" behaved calmly. The nature of the conversation was not like a first encounter after joining the service. He spoke about all questions without reservation: about personnel matters, the correct direction of relations between state and church and the tactics which have to be applied in relation to the congregations.[5]

Bishop Káldy's, aka Pécsi's written reports are very revealing. The young bishop actually took the lead and secretly made personal recommendations that were clearly vital for his new service. He fought on two parallel fronts: trying to overshadow those supporting the anti-Communist Ordass and those further to the left than he, and to express loyalty to the Soviet-oriented state. It was a schizophrenic situation with many question marks: in his human resource policy, the bishop relied on the state security services; moreover, he presented his suggestions under a code name.

Káldy was very interested in international contacts, particularly with the LWF. At the time, Ordass was a Vice-President of the LWF, but could not fulfill his position due to his forced retirement. Nonetheless, the LWF regarded Ordass as the elected Vice-President. This created a tension that never eased, even after Káldy's election as President of the LWF.

Barely three months after Káldy's inauguration, the first official meeting with the leadership of the LWF took place at the Hotel Regina, Vienna, Austria. The LWF sent a high level delegation, presided by the Bishop of New York, Franklin Fry, and including General Secretary Carl Lund-Quist, Bishop Bo Giertz of Goteborg, Bishop Hermann Dietzfelbinger of Munich, pastor Mogens Zeuthen from Denmark and the finance officer, Rudolf Weeber. It is noteworthy that Káldy was accompanied by Miklós Pálfy, dean of the theological academy, who was quasi controlling the bishop "from the left." Fortunately both "Pécsi's" collaborative report and official LWF minutes are available from this meeting. When we read the two texts side by side, we can conclude that Káldy was actually rather fair in his summary of the meeting and its results. Nonetheless, it is bizarre that the bishop would not hand in the report of such a meeting to his church but to the state security services, under a code name. The differences between the report and the minutes are also noteworthy: Káldy does not mention that he commented positively on Ordass. It is difficult to decide whether he was (still) honestly thinking along these lines or was trying to be diplomatic. He also refers to his comments in Vienna when he writes in his report to the authorities:

The leadership of the Evangelical Lutheran Church in Hungary is trying to serve in a way that enables the church to remain a church in Hungary. But the church is taking a special way since under socialism it has to take a new path. In this

---

[5] Ibid., 283.

respect, someone from the West cannot give advice to a church living in the East. The Evangelical Lutheran Church in Hungary wants to promote socialism.[6]

The LWF minutes do not include statements about supporting socialism. There one only finds a church political statement:

> In the church we try to go the way of Christ even under a proletarian dictatorship government. At the same time we want to support what is good in a proletarian dictatorship.[7]

Despite these different emphases, Káldy's report and the LWF minutes are identical in their main points. Therefore, it is even stranger to read the comment by an officer who mistrusts the informer: "The analysis is quite hasty which I also pointed out to the informer. The report does not include everything he told me."[8] The captain from the Ministry of Interior Affairs is also suspicious of the LWF remarking, "The Lutheran World Federation leadership came to the meeting with concrete information."[9]

In his report of 2 July 1962, "Pécsi" outlines the structure of the LWF, its activities and leading figures in great detail. After providing statistical data, the informer describes the LWF's political nature, which must have been the most interesting part for the authorities.[10] He affirms that "As the majority of Lutherans live in the West, the LWF's political nature is defined by a Western orientation."[11] Then he refers to the Western societies' and churches' fear of Communism and talks about the LWF's "constant pain" that Latvian and Estonian Lutherans have "lost their freedom" (he estimates their number to be 500 000 and 350,000 respectively). With reference to Germany, he writes "The Lutheran World Federation cannot accept the division of the country of the Reformation and is always speaking out against it."[12] Here he also hints that the LWF leadership objects to the construction of the Berlin wall. Káldy's main personal problem was that "the LWF's leadership continuously has the so-called Ordass-issue on their agenda. They see in him a hero who has resisted the Communists up

---

[6] Cited in András Korányi, *Hanem szeretni is. Káldy Zoltán püspöki szolgálata itthon és külföldön* [But also to Love: The Service of Bishop Zoltán Káldy at Home and Abroad] (Budapest: Luther Kiadó, 2012), 39–40.

[7] Ibid., 143.

[8] Ibid., 39, footnote 46.

[9] Ibid., 159.

[10] Háló 2, op. cit. (note 4), 313–16

[11] Ibid., 313.

[12] Ibid.

to martyrdom."[13] Since at international negotiations, the LWF's leadership not only stood behind its Vice-President, Ordass, but also questioned the legality of removing Ordass from his position as bishop, Káldy experienced a legitimization deficit. "Pécsi" writes about how Káldy increasingly gained prestige in the LWF and clearly presents the LWF one-sidedly. But, he also intends to increase the Hungarian authorities' trust in the organization. For example, he mentions that among the leadership, there are some anti-Communists but also more enlightened people. He refers to the American Bishop Fry, the Finnish Archbishop Simojoki and Niemöller, concluding that "One cannot say that the LWF is, on the whole, reactionary."[14]

In the following I would like to analyze the difference between the two informers. The analysis will make reference to a prominent person within the LWF, the former Europe secretary, the Dane Paul Hansen. Hansen was familiar with church life behind the iron curtain and visited Hungary several times. In summer 1960, he spent almost two weeks there, participating at church services and ordinations, studying church media and controlling the use of a 100,000 USD grant. The police officer remarked about Hansen's visit, "During his stay, we had him under control through several informers."[15] One of those informers was a professor of theology Ernő Ottlyk, who served as a bishop between 1967 and 1982. He reported to the state security services for decades under the code name "László Szamosi." In his report of 6 July 1960, he analyzes Paul Hansen's personality and activity in Hungary in great detail. He briefly mentions that according to Hansen, there is a living church in Hungary but after that he only provides information likely to pit the authorities against Hansen. He reports in detail on Hansen's critique of church life, especially about the church media, citing the sharp words with which Hansen had criticized the proletarian dictatorship, which he called a totalitarian state. He also quotes Hansen on the absence of political freedom in Hungary. In his report, Ottlyk lists the names of all pastors who had requested a motorcycle from the LWF and finds fault with almost every one of them with regard to their family background, contact with deaconesses or supposedly belonging to Bishop Ordass's circle. In accusing his fellow pastors he presumably caused a great deal of harm.

Bishop Káldy's report of 9 July 1960, gives a totally different evaluation of Paul Hansen. Káldy depicts him in a favorable light. In his report we read, "According to his own words, he is regarded as a 'progressive' pastor in Denmark. [...] His statements in Hungary were overwhelmingly positive."[16] In a sermon

---

[13] Ibid., 314.
[14] Ibid., 316.
[15] Ibid., 299.
[16] Ibid., 298

Hansen held in Budapest, he stated that "the main topic was the nuclear threat and its possible solutions." Káldy underlines that due to his diplomatic efforts, Hansen did not visit Bishop Ordass. "Although he wanted to visit Ordass, he gave up the plan after Káldy told him that it would not be good and would harm the relations between the LWF and the Evangelical Lutheran Church in Hungary." [17]

It is worth looking at how the two informers—"Pécsi" and "László Szamosi"—report about one another. Both of them were bishops of the same church, together serving in their respective positions for fifteen years. Ottlyk referred to Káldy and his circle as the "rescuers of the church," which, at the time, was anything but positive. He believed Káldy to have tactics "to rescue the church and its reactionary forces through a progressive sounding voice." [18] When Káldy prepared for marriage, Ottlyk remarks rather unpleasantly, that "Káldy is very much in love. Because of the marriage, he will deal less with the church and will be more submissive." [19] Since Káldy married the daughter of the Reformed lay leader Tamás Esze, Ottlyk assumed that the bishop would regularly exchange political views with his father-in-law and work toward strengthening the relationship between the two churches which, in the Communist environment, was not welcome. Káldy's plans to reduce church administration are outlined in the collaborative report of his future colleague:

> From a formal point of view, it may seem positive that he wants to introduce the rules of the socialist state in the church. In substance however, it is a reactionary step that makes the structure of the church more up-to-date and introduces discipline and professionalism to where there used to be anarchy before. As much as disciplined work, professionalism and planned operation are required in state administration, it is unnecessary in the church as it will only strengthen the church. [20]

Is this the voice of a church person?

There are examples where "Pécsi" reports on "Szamosi." Káldy was aware of the fact that, for the state (and the state security services) Ottlyk was the more trustworthy source. Therefore he was careful and restrained in his criticism. For example, in connection with his participation at the Helsinki LWF Assembly: "[Ottlyk] was quiet. All members of the Hungarian delegation remarked that and they criticized the inactivity of Ottlyk among themselves." [21] When Ottlyk, already as a bishop, participated at a

---

[17] Ibid., 298–99.
[18] Cited in ibid., 472.
[19] Ibid.
[20] Ibid., 473.
[21] Ibid., 456.

conference of European minority Lutheran churches in 1968, Káldy reported that, "Bishop Ottlyk did not say a word once. This gave reason for much speculation among the others."[22]

The Lutheran church leader with the code name László Szamosi (or should we rather say: the collaborative agent with a pseudo position as a professor of theology and a bishop) was not merely characterized by quietness. In his report of 24 August 1963, Ottlyk mentions the Hungarian pastor Vilmos Vajta, who lived in Geneva and whom he regarded as the ideologist behind the LWF. He described Vajta with the following words:

> From the personal perspective, he leaves an impression of a rootless, unsettled man. He declares himself Hungarian but is a Swedish citizen, his wife is Swedish but they live in Geneva and the children are raised in a linguistic chaos. He tries to survive this situation with the help of cosmopolitan views. Among the church-related Hungarian emigrants, only Vajta has made a career. In his rootless situation, his dignity is maintained by dollars only.[23]

NEED FOR FURTHER SELF-EXAMINATION AND REPENTANCE: SO THAT THE PAST MAY BE FORGIVEN

In my opinion, there is still much to do with regard to the activities of the LWF and its member churches during the Cold War. Personally I would find the research on the secret service coverage of the 1984 Budapest Assembly highly relevant. It would also be interesting to relate the ongoing research programs to the findings of the South African Truth and Reconciliation program, since I believe there to be many similarities: the lack of freedom and the fact that many people were deprived of their rights, their humanity and their dignity. Both systems also had its beneficiaries—the oppressors themselves and those who tried to escape hardship by committing vicious acts. Not everybody could accept suffering and the cross of Christ. Thinking of younger generations, we often speak about "the grace of having being born late." This may be true but we never know when the church and each individual Christian might have to face a situation where an attitude of confessing is needed. Researching the past does not only serve to educate but it may turn out to prepare us for what lies ahead of us.

I believe the recognition of the past in the Evangelical Lutheran Church in Hungary to be especially important for several reasons. It may serve as an example for the whole Central Eastern Europe region (or even in a wider

---

[22] Ibid.
[23] Ibid., 603.

perspective) for understanding that a community has to face its own past and its own sins. At the same time, we must follow the apostle's word, "If one member suffers, all suffer together" (1 Cor 12:26). The sin of the other is my sin, the pain of the other is my pain. This biblical approach also helps to shift the emphasis from the political to the ethical aspect.

We know how difficult it is to confess the past. In many cases, we are faced with personal tragedies and it is crucial that during the whole process of reviewing the past we not only protect personal rights but also act according to Luther's understanding of the Eighth Commandment, namely to "not tell lies about our neighbors [...] or destroy their reputations. Instead we are to [...] speak well of them".[24] Furthermore, we should not punish, stigmatize and humiliate future generations because of their parents' deeds. But we have to speak about the issue. Recognition, research and confession of the past are relevant for us and our Christian vocation.

Archive documents that shed light on this rather dark period should be published. This is also true for church documents, which must be published in a way that avoids the risk of falsification.

In addition to factual archive material, there is space for personal accounts about how someone was roped into collaborating—be it in the 1950s or 1980s. Through this, one can also learn about counter-espionage. In the Evangelical Lutheran Church in Hungary we encourage people to speak. Many people live with great burdens and some think that their secrets should not be made public. Recognizing the past becomes not only an historical but a theological and pastoral challenge. Speaking up and starting a conversation may prove therapeutic. One could also speak about unsuccessful and successful attempts to rope someone into collaborating and about oral and written reports. We can speak about sins that even the documents fail to capture and just as we repeat in the liturgy of confession in our church we repeat, "I confess" ... "I repent" ... "I've been forgiven/I have forgiven".

All this requires self-examination. We do not have to stand before sometimes self-appointed prosecutors and judges but before the living God. The church can only face its own past if it chooses to do so not because of external pressure but internal motivation. Not alone but in the community of the church.

According to Dietrich Bonhoeffer the church must not remain silent. Rather it must take responsible action in society and ready to suffer for what is acknowledged as right. However, when the church confesses to

---

[24] Martin Luther, "The Small Catechism," in Robert Kolb and Timothy J. Wengert (eds), *The Book of Concord. The Confessions of the Evangelical Lutheran Church* (Minneapolis: Fortress Press, 2000), 353.

having remained silent, this does not exempt the people from their own confession. Rather, it invites them to the community of confession.

Today, our churches have to strive to speak and to act. This implies an honest encounter with our past. Not by washing one's dirty linen in public but by accepting a shared responsibility for a common issue. Researching the past must be guided by the principle of truth in love. Although members of our committee try to act carefully and considerately, the results of the research must be published, including the real names, not just the code names given to the informers by the state security services. The members of the research committee have informed several church leaders and pastors past and present that their collaboration can be proven with evidence from the archives. The members of the committee underlined in each case there were different motivations for and forms of collaboration. The frequency of the reports, the topics included, the value of the information and the impact of the report on other people's lives differ widely.

Recognition of the past must be accompanied by constant prayer. Through asking again and again, "forgive us our debts, as we also have forgiven our debtors" (Mt 6:12). Jesus is resolute in saying, "Your sins are forgiven" (Mk 2:5) and also when he asks, "Father, forgive them; for they do not know what they are doing" (Lk 23:34). Moses prays in an intercession for his nation, "But now, if you will only forgive their sin—but if not, blot me out of the book that you have written" (Ex 32:32).

I would like to conclude with a text by the Hungarian poet János Pilinszky. In his *Könyörgés a csalókért* (Intercession for tricksters), he writes:

I feel deep sympathy for cardsharpers who are never able to face themselves and their deeds. In comparison to them, a murderer who has assessed his deed and suffered for it is at once a lamb and a glorious victim. But what is it like to live with black, sweaty nails, in an atmosphere of "eternal falsehood"? It is a fate worse than a hit man's. Murderers at least cannot keep hiding their sins from themselves, even only if on their deathbed. But the small trickster, the petty manipulator—be it under his own name or an alias— usually gets off lightly. [...] This is the real tragedy. Great sins are purifying just as the electric chair. But what can such a sinner hope for who commits his sin in a petty, watchful way? He will probably get off the pains of life but deprives himself of all its sensations. Us, the decayed may at least inhale our death into our lungs but what will remain of him? We are dirty. He is smeary. Sloven, to put it right. What could I wish for him? To be hot. Or to be cold. But he is already used to being lukewarm.[25]

---

[25] http://www.ekor-lap.hu/kultura/2011/konyorges-a-csalokert, author's own translation.

We do not have to be a "smeary" church. Our fate is not to remain in an in-between, lukewarm position. We can create an atmosphere in the Lutheran World Federation and in its member churches where one can say, I ask for forgiveness, both from a human and a godly perspective: I forgive. And we may speak with the credibility of an eyewitness about what we have seen and experienced and we may witness to God who gives us grace and absolution and a new life, transforming and reconciling us with one another.

THEOLOGY AND ECONOMICS

ECONOMY AND GRACE:
A LUTHERAN APPROACH TO
MONEY, RELIGION AND DEBT

Guillermo Hansen

A new specter is haunting our lives—the specter of debt. How is debt related to theology? Luther offers two points of entry: one is his analysis of early capitalist practices during the sixteenth century and the ravaging effect of a debt society; the other is his identification of the reality of money and its instruments not just as an ethical or practical problem, but as a confessional one: "the trust and faith of the heart alone make both God and an idol," Luther remarks in his "Large Catechism," adding that "mammon ... is the most common idol on earth."[1]

In the first part I shall explore Luther's understanding of the early practices of capitalism and to what extent his view can be gauged against Walter Benjamin's thesis regarding capitalism as a "religion." We shall see that Luther approached the matter of money, capital, and debt as the arena for an "apocalyptic" struggle between God and the Devil, a struggle marked by a misplaced and distorted "trust and faith." In the Reformer's view the economy of "gift," represented by Christ, is contrasted with the economy of "debt," the paragon of the demonic.

If for Luther faith meant to "trust in God alone, to look to him alone, and to expect him to give us only good things; for it is he who gives us body, life, food, drink, nourishment, health, protection, peace and all necessary temporal and

---

[1] Martin Luther, "The Large Catechism," in Robert Kolb and Timothy J. Wengert (eds), *The Book of Concord: The Confessions of the Evangelical Lutheran Church* (Minneapolis: Fortress Press, 1959), 387.

eternal blessings,"[2] then for capitalism the seat of all hope is the miraculous quality of money. But if capitalism survives thanks to deep psychological and emotional urges that "make both God or an idol," what should our Christian stance be? In the second part I shall revisit Luther's insight that outlines a threefold strategy for Christian living: living from the end times as shaped by the event of Christ as gift; living between the times as engagement with neighbors and creation; and living at the end of (an historical) time as preparation for a revolutionary bifurcation in history. From, between and at the end of times thus mark the proper Christian existence, an existence that is critical of current economic practices and conceptions (cynical living),[3] eagerly expectant of the new to come (revolutionary living), and yet engaged in a permanent deferral of the final apocalyptic denouement in history for the sake of creation (reformist living). Luther's views on the three orders of creation and the twofold governance of God allow us to encompass the three aspects listed above in a powerful anti-fragile[4] recipe in the midst of the fragile texture of history.

LUTHER AND CAPITAL

For Luther, money, debt and labor were theological issues of the first order, referring to relational fields in which and through which the struggle between the Devil and Christ was carried out.[5] Not only was he a keen observer and analyst of the early manifestations of what later came to be known as "capitalism," but he identified practices such as credit, debt, inflation, interest, usury, rent, and monopoly as expressions of unbelief,

---

[2] Ibid., 389.

[3] I employ the term "cynical" to refer to a critical attitude to prevailing values and practices grounded in the realization of the desires of the ego. In this sense, cynical refers to the unmasking of selfishness—individual and collective.

[4] I borrow the notion of "antifragility" from Nassim Nicholas Taleb, *Antifragile: Things that Gain from Disorder* (New York: Random House, 2012). Taleb claims that "antifragility is beyond resilience or robustness. The resilient resists shocks and stays the same; the antifragile gets better." The task, therefore, is not to attack fragility at its root (for that would deprive life of its stressors, i.e., its viability), but "the reduction of fragility or harnessing antifragility" (Kindle Edition, locations 339, 353, 361).

[5] Cf. Oswald Bayer, *Martin Luther's Theology: A Contemporary Interpretation* (Grand Rapids: Wm. B. Eerdmans, 2008), 2–5. Also, Heiko Oberman, *Luther: Man between God and the Devil* (New York: Doubleday, 1989), 102–106. Oberman writes: "Luther's world of thought is wholly distorted and apologetically misconstrued if his conception of the Devil is dismissed as a medieval phenomenon and only his faith in Christ retained as relevant or as the only decisive factor. Christ and the Devil were equally real to him: one was the perpetual intercessor for Christianity, the other a menace to mankind till the end. . . . Christ and the Satan wage a cosmic war for mastery over Church and world" (104).

a demonic reality, even Satan's kingdom.[6] "Money," Luther writes, "is the word of the Devil, through which he creates all things the way God created through the true word."[7] Economic as well as political issues were theological fields in which not only the individual engages with nature and other human beings in productive and distributive spheres, but areas where God's very work was at stake. "Creatures are only the hands, channels, and means through which God bestows all blessings," Luther states in his "Large Catechism."[8] And in his Confession of 1528 he propounds a theology of three "holy orders" (household/economy, secular government, church) through which we are engaged in God's holy work.[9]

For us better to understand the place that the economy in general, and "capitalism" in particular, had in Luther, we will follow an oblique path provided by one of Walter Benjamin thesis: "One can behold in capitalism a religion, that is to say, capitalism essentially serves to satisfy the same worries, anguish, and disquiet formerly answered by so-called religion."[10] Benjamin does not explicitly state that capitalism is a religion, but rather that in capitalism we can discern one of the structuring principles of religion. The kernel of religion, according to Benjamin, is *Schuld* (guilt)—a dual sign that implies both guilt in the religious, moral sense, and debt in the economic sense.[11] For Benjamin, capitalism "makes [*Schuld*] pervasive. Capitalism is probably the first instance of a cult that creates [*Schuld*], not atonement."[12] This is a critical observation because if the basic structure

---

[6] See Ricardo Rieth, "Luther on Greed," in *Lutheran Quarterly* XV/3 (Autumn 2001), 345. See also Martin Brecht, *Martin Luther: The Preservation of the Church (1532-1546)*, transl. James Schaaf (Minneapolis: Fortress Press, 1999), 259f. I will follow Tillich's interpretation of the demonic as the perversion and destruction of the structures of creation.

[7] *WA Tischreden*, I Band, #391 (170). Cf. Mark C. Taylor, *After God* (Chicago: The University of Chicago Press, 2007), 64.

[8] *BC*, 389.

[9] See Martin Luther, "Confession Concerning Christ's Supper," in Timothy Lull (ed.), *Martin Luther's Basic Theological Writings*, second edition (Minneapolis: Fortress Press, 2005), 65.

[10] Walter Benjamin, "Capitalism as Religion," in *Selected Writings*, vol. 1, 259. Text accessed at http://www.complit.u-szeged.hu/images/benjamin_-_capitalism_as_religion.pdf

[11] As indicated by the Greek term *opheilemata* (debt) in Matthew's version of the Lord's Prayer (Mt 6:12), in distinction from Luke (Lk 11:4) were debts are replaced by sins (*hamartias*). See Robert Funk (ed.), *The Five Gospels: The Search for the Authentic Words of Jesus* (New York: HarperCollins, 1997), 149, 326.

[12] I follow here the translation offered by Daniel Weidner, "Thinking beyond Secularization: Walter Benjamin, the 'Religious Turn', and the Poetics of Theory," in *New German Critique* 111, vol. 37, no. 3 (Fall 2010), 140.

of religion is *Schuld* (i.e., debt compounded by guilt), then capitalism is a sublime expression of the negative pole of this structure (i.e., it is sustained by the perpetual generation of debt/guilt). Yet the lack of any atonement converts it into an utterly demonic religion, "an order, whose sole constitutive concepts are misery and guilt and in which there is no way of liberation." A religion without atonement or liberation is what characterizes the historical "enormity" of capitalism. In this instance, "Religion is no longer the reform of being, but rather its obliteration."[13]

Did Luther regard "capitalism" as a religion? Certainly he never referred to "capitalism" in these terms, since what today we understand as such is a category gained through historical hindsight. But he did indeed address a host of new practices that later were deemed to be the early expressions of the "capitalist" mode of production and accumulation. Luther had a concept of religion that was able to locate the phenomena of early capitalist practices, not just as an anomaly in the smooth texture of the feudal world but as the structuring of subjectivities in open discord with the Christian faith.

CAPITALISM: A RELIGION? REVISITING THE FIRST COMMANDMENT

Let us turn to a minimalist definition of religion that we find in Luther. Religion is a matter not just captured by a certain cosmology, institutional arrangement, not even a previous definition of a metaphysical transcendence, but it is lodged in what Luther calls faith as trust: an anthropological phenomenon that structures human existence. This is clearly seen in Luther's commentary on the first commandment in the "Large Catechism." We know very well his introductory remarks that set in tandem God, heart, and faith:

> to have a god is nothing else than to trust and believe in that one with your whole heart. As I have often said, it is the trust and faith of the heart alone that make both God and an idol. If your faith and trust are right, then your God is the true one. Conversely, where your trust is false and wrong, there you do not have the true God. For these two belong together, faith and God. Anything on which you heart relies and depends, I say, that is really your God.[14]

Yet we often forget the following counter-example given by Luther:

> There are some who think that they have God and everything they need when they have money and property; they trust in them and boast so stubbornly and securely that he cares for no one else. They, too, have a god—mammon by name,

---

[13] Benjamin, op. cit. (note 10), 260.
[14] *BC*, 386.

that is, money and property—on which they set their whole heart. This is the most common idol on earth. Those who have money and propertay feel secure, happy, an fearless, as if they were sitting in the midst of paradise. On the other hand, those who has nothing doubt and despair as if they knew no god at all. We will find very few who are cheerful, who do not fret and complain, if they do not have mammon. The desire for wealth clings and sticks to our nature all the way to the grave.[15]

After expounding on other examples, Luther concludes that these forms of idolatry do not "consist merely of erecting an image and praying to it, but it is primarily a matter of the heart, which fixes its gaze upon other things and seeks help and consolation from creatures, saints, or devils." [16] Two things need to be noted here. In the first place, Luther employs the category of "heart" as a metonymy for the subjective dimension of the human being.[17] At the same time, this subjectivity is materially and historically mediated, "produced" through the different relational fields in which persons are implicated. These relational fields or spheres are what Luther calls "orders"—orders that always serve as channels for trust.

What today we term "capitalism" Luther perceived not so much as a new form of economic and social organization, but as a new spiritual and material force in complete dissonance with Christianity—an idolatry. In other words, a new structuring of hearts and bodies based on the "religious" premise that something (e.g., money, profit) can be made out of nothing. Luther placed the problem of money making squarely within the confession of the first commandment: capitalism is trusting in oneself and making oneself God, "for whatever a man trusts in and relies upon is his god."[18] Capitalism, thus, can be regarded as a religion, albeit a false one.

LUTHER'S THEOLOGICAL AND PASTORAL APPROACH
TO EARLY CAPITALIST PRACTICES

Besides his classical "Trade and Usury (1524)," and the "Admonition to the Clergy to Preach Against Usury (1540)," economic references traverse much of Luther's exegetical, pastoral, and theological writings. One should regard his explicit allusions against capitalist practices as an extension of his initial confrontation with the abuse of indulgences and the scholastic pattern of thought. Thus there are at least two moments—which increas-

---

[15] Ibid., 387.
[16] Ibid., 388.
[17] See Tuomo Mannermaa, *Two Kinds of Love: Martin Luther's Religious World*, transl. Kirsi Stjerna (Minneapolis: Fortress Press, 2010), 5f.
[18] Martin Luther, "Trade and Usury (1540)," in *LW* 45, 254.

ingly overlapped as the Reformation unfolded—that concentrate Luther's address of the problem of "capitalism." The first moment, often misunderstood as merely a critique of church abuses, constitutes a veritable *casus confessionis* that was geared not against the papacy as such, but against the tyranny of a new logic and practice within the church.

In criticizing indulgences, the mass, and the scholastic paradigm of nature and grace, Luther questioned a logic that mimicked new economic practices. In the medieval church the most precious of religious goods—the forgiveness of sins—had become a monetized commodity mediated by the practices of indulgences and penance. In 1343, Pope Clement VI gave a "capitalist" turn to the belief and practices of indulgences by claiming that the wide distribution of heavenly treasure would lead to an increase in merit, which, in turn, continued the accumulation of wealth in a sort of virtuous cycle.[19] In addition, the house of the Hohenzoller's had incurred an enormous debt to the powerful Fugger bankers and the income from the sale of indulgences was to be equally distributed to the creditor, the Fugger, and the "owner" of the proprietary rights, Rome. Thus Luther's attack on indulgences simultaneously addressed, *in obliquo,* the "capitalistic" logic that had seeped into the church's practice and theology. In effect, the whole reproach against work-righteousness was an attack on the very idea of a *Schuld* that can and must be repaid by the sinner-debtor.

Luther addressed the captivity of the economy and the compliance of the state to the mythological power of money and debt. While quipping about material wealth, usury, interests, avarice, and greed had been a staple in the vitriol of Franciscans and Dominicans for centuries, Luther goes beyond the moralistic aspect that simply treats money with contempt in order to redirect believers towards higher "spiritual" values. He can and does condemn in the harshest words usurers and merchants: "Merchants can hardly be without sin (Eccl 26:29), the love of money is the root of all evils (1 Tim 6:10)"[20] or "Merchants think they are gods."[21] But then he moves further by unlocking the mystifying qualities of money as resting in the exploitation of the neighbor's losses, needs, wants, and labor. "You cannot make money just with money,"[22] Luther notes, underscoring the perverse machinations undergirding a new sphere of exchanges, the capitalist market.

In a revealing passage Luther describes the mechanism of profit-seeking and exploitation:

---

[19] See Erik Erikson, *Young Man Luther: A Study in Psychoanalysis and History* (New York: Norton, 1958), 188.

[20] *LW* 45, 246.

[21] Ibid., 248.

[22] Ibid., 299.

> When once the rogue's eye and greedy belly of a merchant find that people must have his wares, or that the buyer is poor and needs them, he takes advantage of him and raises the price. He considers not the value of the goods, or what his own efforts and risk have deserved, but only the other man's want and need … . Because of his avarice, therefore, the goods must be priced as much higher as the greater need of the other fellow will allow, so that the neighbor's need becomes as it were the measure of the good's worth and value.

And indignantly asks:

> Tell me, isn't that an un-Christian and inhuman thing to do? Isn't that the equivalent to selling a poor man his own need in the same transaction? When he has to buy his wares at a higher price because of his need, that is the same as having to buy his own need; for what is sold to him is not simply the wares as they are, but the wares *plus* the fact that he must have them.[23]

But while want and need may explain the occasion for the profit of the merchant, it does not yet describe the source for enacting the exchange between buyer and seller. That, for Luther, is the buyer's labor that provides the surplus of value or profit. The capitalist "sucks up the other's blood and sweat."[24]

Commenting on Luther's sermon, the historian Gerhard Brendler points out that,

> [F]or the first time in the history of economic thought Luther exposed the fact that the creditor purchased the work of the borrower and that the interest on the money lent did not come out of some magic power of money or from the natural fertility of a mortgaged farm: **it came from the work of the borrower**.[25]

Karl Marx credits Luther with this novel insight, and quotes him at length to disprove the notion of "the idea of capital as a self-reproducing and thereby self expanding value, lasting and growing eternally by virtue of its inherent power."[26]

Luther's diatribes against the early practices of capitalism are further developed in two areas: one is the proper Christian attitude towards it, firmly

---

[23] Ibid., 248.

[24] Ibid., 309.

[25] Gerhard Brendler, *Martin Luther: Theology and Revolution*, transl. Claude R. Foster, Jr. (New York, Oxford: Oxford University Press, 1991), 162, author's own emphasis.

[26] Karl Marx, *Capital: A Critique of Political Economy*, vol III, The Process of Capitalist Production as a Whole, transl. Ernest Untermann (Chicago: Charles H. Kerr & Co., 1909), 461–63.

rooted in the parenetic dimension of the gospel that for the Christian, as a bearer of Christ, does not come as an external demand or law but flows forth as a spontaneous act of love elicited by the neighbor in need.[27] His injunctions as to how goods ought to be exchanged by Christians may sound naïve, but it spells out the proper form of exchange—in principle applicable to all spheres of human existence—as patterned by the "exchange" between God and humanity enacted in Christ: here the "debtor" (the sinner) is met not by the demands of the "Great Creditor" (God), but by God's own self-giving. It is God's own "Self," namely Christ, which is given as a free gift in lieu of the lack that traverses humanity's very being. In sum, God's own economy coincides with God's own unfolding where God does not demand repayment in the sense of a "fair" exchange between human virtues and good works for God's grace and salvation. On the contrary, the very rules of a "fair" exchange are abolished. This is the "happy exchange,"[28] a cornerstone of Luther's entire theology, which in turn shapes the exchange of Christians with one another and the world.

The Reformer believed that confessing Christ implied, in the material realm of exchanges of God's gifts, an engagement with one or all of the four "Christian ways of exchanging external goods with others":[29] to let the other steal our property, to give freely to anyone who needs it, to lend without expecting anything in return, and to exchange goods through the buying and selling for cash or payment in kind.[30] In other words, Christian communities are imagined as spaces of "communist" practices, where exchanges and commerce are not ruled by the logic of endless profit through the financial mechanisms of surety, interest based credit, and selling commodities "as dear as one can."[31]

Luther knows that those who are ruled by the gospel, although robust in faith, are left in a "fragile" situation in the spheres of exchange, vulnerable to every type of abuse and injustice. Although the gospel is robust in its ability to transform subjects and create community, it is fragile as a means for ordering the whole of society. The gospel can neither compel nor enforce its injunctions onto those whose subjectivity and practices are captive to other "gods." Thus Luther's understanding of the role of law and secular authority serves as a necessary "anti-fragile" strategy. The

---

[27] As the opening remarks of his "Long Sermon on Usury" indicates: "Therefore, it is necessary in these perilous times for everyone to be alert, to use proper discretion in dealing with the temporal goods, paying diligent attention to the holy gospel of Christ our Lord." *LW* 45, 273.

[28] See Martin Luther, "The Freedom of a Christian," in Lull, op. cit. (note 9), 397.

[29] *LW* 45, 255.

[30] Ibid., 256–59.

[31] Ibid., 261.

fact that Christians are rare, and that the world is still God's good creation despite being held captive by sin, led Luther to expound on a theology of the three orders and two regiments as an antidote to abuse, exploitation, and injustice for the sake of creation as a whole. We shall return to this below.

SCHULD, WORK-RIGHTEOUSNESS AND GIFT: THE CONFLICT OF CODES

By measuring Luther's thinking in light of Walter Benjamin theses, one can risk the following conclusions:

- As Benjamin maintains, the new economic practices described and criticized by Luther can be theologically approached as manifestations of the basic structure of a religion grounded in *Schuld*. Luther's initial confrontation with Rome had little to do with cosmetic reforms of religious practices and liturgy, but with a cancellation of the classical "sacrificial" economy of signs where the human subject is always in debt with the "provider"—which ensued in the well-known scheme of works and the selling of indulgences. This theological economy created a perpetual state of indebtedness where the more grace was poured, the more of a debtor one became. This scheme provided the theological template for the legitimization of new monetary practices—one where creditor and debtor, God and sinner, are engaged in a (capitalist) transactional scheme. The scholastic version of Christianity erected a system of objects where signs could be exchanged like commodities (i.e., virtues for grace). Hence Luther's theological injunctions against capitalist practices were forged not merely by an ethical indignation, but also by a theological reversal of a system of exchangeable and negotiable signs by a code based on Christ as gift. Hence his attack on church practices (indulgences), scholasticism (work righteousness), and "capitalism" (indebtedness): all are different expressions of the same structuring code.

- The cancellation of this economy of signs is theologically enacted by Luther's transformation of the code of exchange. He introduces an economy of symbols that is based in the reality of a gift. The paramount expression of this shift is embedded in his theology of the cross where the *fröhliche Wechsel* gives something (Christ) in lieu of nothing (sin, debt). This implies a total remittance of Schuld, thus breaking a (demonic) mechanism of asymmetries. The articulation of the law-gospel modes of addressing the human situation expresses this: while the law teaches what we ought to do, the gospel teaches what we ought to receive; while the law is the taskmaster that demands that we work and that we give, the gospel grants freely and only commands to receive what it is offered. Thus, "If the Gospel is a gift and offers a gift, it does not demand anything."[32]

- Capitalist practices are an embodiment of self-seeking gain, in direct opposition to Christ's (and the Christian's) self-giving presence. It is an infringement of the first commandment by centering one's whole self and one's whole personality not only on earthly realities, which lack ultimacy and cannot fulfill the human vocation, but also on the active exploitation of the neighbor's needs and wants.

- Finally, from Luther's perspective, "capitalism" can be considered as a (demonic) religion in that it replicates in the secular domain the same logic found in a church dominated by the "anti-Christ." It is grounded, indeed, in "faith," but a faith that "disrupts" personality (Tillich) and eschews the whole social fabric of existence. In short, it is grounded in a mechanism of dispossession.

We now need to explore Luther's distinction between the three orders and two regiments as a strategy able to deal with evil and abuse.

LUTHER'S ANTI-FRAGILE STRATEGY: THREE SIMULTANEOUS WAYS OF CHRISTIAN LIVING

If the foregoing analysis is correct, both the efficacy and appeal of money is grounded in the old religious axiom of *Schuld*—guilt and debt. The problem is therefore twofold. On the one hand, the predicament of the signification and representation of subjectivity, on the other, how the inherent fragility can be contained in its deleterious social effects without the recourse to totalitarian or oppressive measures. With that we enter into the structural-ethical problem.

THE APOCALYPSE OF GOD, FAITH AND THE SELF: LIVING FROM THE END OF TIMES

Christianity approaches the first problem, the subject shackled to *Schuld*, through a radical understanding of faith as an apocalyptic event taking place in the chain of significations that constitute the subject as such. This marks an end, yet also a beginning. It is marked by a struggle between ego and a new self (Christ) as expounded in Paul's enigmatic words in Galatians 2:20:

---

[32] Martin Luther, "Lecture on Galatians (1535)," in *LW* 26, 208–209.

"and it is no longer I who live, but it is Christ who lives in me."[33] Righteousness and faith are not the outcome of hard work on the basis of our substantial potentialities and attributes, but the acceptance and integration of an "alien" perspective in the very symbolic web that constitutes subjectivity.

The understanding of subjectivity as a symbolic and perspectival event implies that we do not possess a substantial reality called "ego" or "consciousness," which produces symbols, but consciousness as such is the result of symbolic linkages. The ego and consciousness are thus a virtual world that in Paul's and Luther's case comprises a battlefield where an old historical trajectory (sin addressed by law) dies and a new life begins (faith in Christ). For Luther, Paul's statement "and it is no longer I who live, but it is Christ" is the center of his proclamation of the righteousness of Christ—a righteousness by which Christ lives in us granting a new symbolic perspectival stance.

It is clear that Christ's righteousness denotes not only a forensic event, but an existential and psychological transition by which an "alien" life is lived as one's own. Christ is the symbol for a new social and relational reinscription of the person, a symbolic order that is unanchored from a world that pits the person against their own ego, other egos, and God. Ego is eminently relational, but it is trapped in the wrong set of perspectives by virtue of a faulty symbolic articulation.

Paul's expression "and it is no longer I who live, but it is Christ who lives in me" implies for Luther a new environment that literally rearranges the phenomenal self of the Christian. But in doing so, it unleashes a new identity that is expressed in the praxis of living. Not only Christ "is fixed and cemented to me and abides in me" in a "virtual" way, but Christ is also the name for the transition between virtuality and actuality, since, "The life that I now live, He lives in me. Indeed, Christ Himself is the life that I now live...."[34] Christ forms the very life that one now lives, a new environment that is disclosed when one is pulled out of one's "own skin." All of Christ attributes—grace, righteousness, life, peace and salvation— are now "cemented" to one's own existence. When one divides one's own person from Christ's, one falls back into the old environment, that of the law and the power of the demonic.

The issue at its root is shifting the code of consumption and debt to that of the gift. It creates a liberated environment where one is free to love the

[33] For Luther's understanding of faith in view of Paul's letter to the Galatians, see Guillermo Hansen, "Luther's Radical Conception of Faith: God, Christ, and Personhood in a Post-Metaphysical Age," in *Dialog: A Journal of Theology* 52/3 (Fall 2013), 212–21.
[34] *LW* 26, 167.

neighbor without falling into the mechanisms of *Schuld,* without seeking to "consume" the other on the basis of their debt and guilt. This freedom elicited by faith turns the subject outwardly in a twofold manner: as a giving praxis in the midst of needs and wants, and thus as a "cynical" critique of the selfish motivations that structure daily life and the prevailing ideology informing our culture. Yet this praxis is grounded in a total passivity, one that results from the new perspectival stance where God comes to us not as the Big Creditor but as a gift. This movement is redoubled in the life of the Christian as the death of an old ego, its semiotic web, and the birth of the new self. This is the strategy that Luther called "spiritual," living from the end times shaped by the event of Christ as a gift. In other words, it outlines a new political economy of the gift, received and embodied in renewed subjects gathered in that community we call church.

LUTHER'S CONCEPTION OF THE THREE ORDERS AND TWO REGIMES: LIVING BETWEEN THE TIMES

Yet Luther was aware that this transformation of the subject is never completed in this life, and, furthermore, that the radical appeal of the gospel has a limited reach. The "gospelling"[35] of human existence through the economy of the gift does not provide the efficacious means to govern a world that is crisscrossed by forces that are structured around egos. This leads to a second strategy, which Luther developed in his theology of the "three orders" and "two regiments" as God's own indefinite deferral of the final apocalyptic fulfillment. This strategy incorporates the former one, yet places it within the historical tension of living between times where God shares the stage with the demonic. The demonic cannot be unswervingly obliterated without endangering God's own creation, yet it can indirectly be restrained, contained, and even sapped of its energies. And while the economy is the ultimate abode of the demonic, it is the political that is able to restrain its venom—or let it loose in the veins of society! This is the "secular," anti-fragile strategy developed by Luther, which corresponds to an existence placed between the times.

First, let us note how this living between the times or "reformist" strategy fares in the face of capitalism. It is well known that Luther horizontalized the classical medieval hierarchical and organic distinction between *ecclesia* (church), *politia* (public realm), and *oeconomia* (household) by decoupling them from distinct castes or classes. All human beings participate in these spheres and institutions. Vítor Westhelle has demonstrated how the Aristotelian categories of *poiesis* and *praxis* may have informed Luther's

---

[35] See Robert Bertram, *A Time for Confessing*, ed. Michael Hoy (Grand Rapids: Wm. B. Eerdmans, 2008), 138.

conception of the range of human activities comprised by the spheres of economy and politics. While *poiesis* denotes an activity whose outcome is the production of something, praxis refers to an intersubjective effect that does not necessarily result in a "material" outcome.

The economy is the realm of the forces that seeks to provide the means for the sustenance and reproduction of life. The political, on the other hand, comprises the sphere of intersubjective relations of production, which "constitutes itself as explanatory narrative and public communication"–the medium of human communicative action, moral deliberation, and juridical legislation.[36] While *poiesis* (economy) deals directly with the conditions that allow for the creation, sustenance and the reproduction of human life, *praxis* (politics) deals directly with the virtual/symbolic conditions that regulate the exchange among human beings. Both are realms of power, yet they function differently. The church, however, distinguishes itself from the other two spheres in that humanity does not produce anything here, no activity of self-representation is enacted. In this instance, our mode of being is not that of action, but that of re-action,[37] namely, our response to God's address, which is both virtual (Word) and material (sacraments).

The reality of abuse (i.e., sin) gives a clear institutional format to the three orders, erecting powerful barriers against (a) the domination of one sphere over the other; (b) the abusive domination within each sphere; and (c) the indiscriminate conversion of one dominant good into another. The common denominator of these three instances is "fragility." Luther's proposal thus addresses the reality and effects of sin in a way that allows a society to avoid succumbing to messianic and totalitarian adventures that would almost certainly attempt to intervene violently to erase the traces of life's fragility.

Second, our perspectives on the pluralistic environment in which we live today, compounded by the single rule of capital undermining every other sphere, can gain from Luther's distinction between the "spiritual" and the "secular." Since capitalism should be seen as a (demonic) religion, we can regard the church as being engaged in a perspectival spiritual-semiotic struggle stemming from another "point of view." It is a struggle between faith in the God of Israel and faith in mammon, between belief and unbelief. In short, this is the battle around the fabrication of "figures of subjectivity" that is always intertwined with the "vicinities of *poiesis* and *praxis*."[38]

The "demythologization" of capitalism is the present struggle of the church, for it is always bound to clash with other "technologies of the self,"

[36] Vitor Westhelle, *The Church Event: Call and Challenge of a Church Protestant* (Minneapolis: Fortress Press, 2010), 33.
[37] Ibid., 40.
[38] Ibid., 41ff.

particularly with those centered in the self-production through the dispossession of other selves. Thus the simple proclamation of the Word to our "hearts" always has an effect on the spheres that our bodies occupy. This is the political and economic *munus* (office, service) and *usus* (use, exercise, practice) of the gospel. Thus no church can be said to be preaching the gospel today without addressing the problem of the idolatrous faith of capitalism. This is a "spiritual" struggle with political and economic effects, for it redraws the foundation of *Schuld* and the pattern of exchange. It is the announcement of a gift and thus the confession that we do not believe in the market; we believe otherwise, in Christ. This is the new "atheistic" face of Christianity, which creates a space where we are given permission not to "enjoy," not to be "happy," not have to explore all our "potentialities" of desire insofar as these are dictated by the capitalist sign-system. This is freedom.

At the same time the struggle and tension is not apart from but within the other spheres comprising our lives. Here the struggle is not directly against capitalism per se, but against its tyranny grounded in the concept of endless profits. Hence the problem is not the market as such, or the place of money within it—the problem is when the criteria of distribution within the market (i.e., money in exchange for goods and services) becomes the criteria that rules in all spheres. Thus the main focus is neither the economy nor the church, but the public sphere, the realm of the commons, governance (*politia*). Luther saw in the government the means for restraining the effects of sin and evil in society (neither *oeconomia* nor *ecclesia* possess the direct means for that). Certainly the political sphere and its institutions do not have the means to produce "good" people—only the gospel can do that.[39] Neither does it possess the means for the production and reproduction of life. But it does have the means that allow for societal welfare.

During the last few decades we have witnessed an erosion of both the legitimacy of the state, political parties, and democratically elected representatives, as well as the active involvement of (democratic) governments in the very setting up of the rules, institutions, and powers of neoliberal globalization. Against the template of Luther's theology of the two governances and three orders it becomes apparent how important the role of the state is and how crucial the "re-enchantment" of the political sphere becomes at this time. Politics, broadly construed, is the only place that can furnish the mechanisms for controlling the anarchic forces of the market. In other words, only *praxis* can create the institutional sphere where *poiesis* can regain its role in the sustainment and reproduction of life. After all, according to Luther's account politics comes into existence

---

[39] Cf. Gustaf Wingren, *Creation and Law* (Philadelphia: Muhlenberg Press, 1961), 164.

when the economy was affected by sin.[40] But whose politics, which state? History shows us that the state and political parties can easily become prisoners to economic interests when a democratic culture of moral deliberation, social control and protest, falters. The public space constituted by this deliberation and mobilization must debate its moral values and vision, as well as serve as the foundation for a political resolve to curb the impulse of a social and economic powerful minority through a regime of democratic representation.

In the meantime, active social policies that deal with the distribution of income, property, and wealth through a reengineering of tributary criteria and processes are a few of the defining characteristics for a reformist agenda. Wealth and riches must be redistributed among the spheres of health, education and culture—not to mention the environment. But any reformist strategy must tackle the core issue: the regulation of creation and allocation of money that fuels financial imperialism.

BIFURCATIONS: LIVING AT THE END OF (A) TIME

The above is just the description of an anti-fragile strategy that I see implied by Luther's understanding of the three orders as an indefinite deferral of the final apocalyptic occurrence. It is a strategy to live "between the times," in the midst of a tension. Yet living between the times also means that the end of an historical cycle is eventually reached. Thus the challenge is how to be engaged as Christians in a reformist path even while "eagerly expecting" (*apekdechomai*, cf. Gal 5:5; 1 Cor 1:7; Rom 8:19)[41] a revolutionary overhaul that can embrace the *kairos* inscribed in the very apocalyptic being of God—and Christians. This is a third strategy where Christians are ready to embrace an unforeseen event in history in partnership with other neighbors. Within the purview of this strategy socio-political reforms are carried out in preparation for and anticipation of an event that can neither be foreseen nor predicted in all its details. The practices of equality, fair taxation, redistribution of income, freedom, sustainability, open access to the commons, etc., form the scaffolding on which, in the event of a radical break in history, a new "ordering" of global society can develop. The centering of subjectivities in the apocalypse of God (Christ), both propel a reformist tactic in the here and now while being open—even being eagerly expectant—to a revolutionary event in the near future.

---

[40] See Vitor Westhelle, "Power and Politics in Luther's Theology," in Christine Helmer (ed.), *The Global Luther: A Theologian for Modern Times* (Minneapolis: Fortress Press, 2009), 295.

[41] See James Dunn, *The Theology of Paul the Apostle* (Grand Rapids: Wm. B. Eerdmans, 1998), 311.

Chaos theory may teach us here a very important "apocalyptic" lesson, namely, in any living system, human societies are open systems faced with a bifurcation at one point or another. All indicates that we are in fact approaching such a moment in history. The chronic crises that we face suggest that the main structural problems cannot be resolved within the parameters offered by the system itself. It is only by going outside of and beyond the historical system that these crises can be minimally resolved. At the brink of bifurcation, it is chaos that dominates, meaning that "every small action during this period is likely to have significant consequences."[42] It is a time where little ripples can become unstoppable waves, where small gestures may have towering repercussions. Thus, our engagement in "reformist" practices—just a collection of temporary measures—are not only important for creating breathing space for those who are suffocated by the market's onslaught, but they are even more critical for providing a template and vectors at the threshold of an impending change. We have a chance for engaging in action and thought that already embodies the irruption of the new.[43]

Finally, the church of Jesus Christ is the "laboratory" of the Spirit, which is to say, it is the location where new perspectival stances and new subjectivities are forged, ready to embrace new trajectories. And here, more than ever, the reversal initiated by Luther, namely, the replacement of an economy of exchangeable signs by an economy of the gift, is at the core of what the proclamation and embodiment of the gospel does: the justification of the indebted by grace alone.[44] Thus, every assembly addressed by the Word, every Lord's Prayer, every exorcism in baptism, and every sharing of the Eucharist, is intrinsically an anti-capitalist practice—despite the particular ideological makeup of those gathered. Echoing CA VII, the pure preaching of the gospel and the correct administration of the sacraments acquires their proper outline against the background of a false gospel and a spurious administration of God's gifts. This is the mind of Christ taking place in ours, establishing its own *oeconomia* through the conformation of a new body (cf. 1 Cor 12). Indeed, the Word effects what it says.[45]

---

[42] Immanuel Wallerstein, *World-Systems Analysis: An Introduction* (Durham: Duke University Press, 2004), 77.

[43] See Franz Hinkelammert, *Cultura de la esperanza y sociedad sin exclusión* (San José, Costa Rica: DEI, 1995), 311.

[44] Cf. the practices regarding debt of an African-American church, Mt. Carmel Baptist Church in Norfolk, VA, documented in the film by Danny Schlechter, *In Debt we Trust* (Altacliff Films, 2006), at http://www.youtube.com/watch?v=TVr813HkEjM .

[45] Cf. Bayer, *op. cit.* (note 5), 52.

The Lord's Prayer as Economic Renewal

Gerald O. West

Introduction

Christian liturgies tend to have domesticated the economic elements of the prayer Jesus taught his disciples—the prayer we refer to as "the Lord's Prayer." Because our churches have chosen to follow Luke's version, we have neglected the economic "argument" of the prayer found in Matthew. As an exercise before reading further, remember for a moment the version of the "Lord's Prayer" that you say in church, in your own language.

Now consider Matthew's version:

> Pray then in this way: Our Father in heaven, hallowed be your name. Your kingdom come. Your will be done, on earth as it is in heaven. Give us this day our daily bread. And forgive us our debts, as we also have forgiven our debtors. And do not bring us to the time of trial, but rescue us from the evil one (Mt 6:9–13).

The version that Matthew has remembered and recorded in these verses is an early version, going back to the time of Jesus and the early church.[1] There is a great deal of biblical scholarship on various aspects of both Matthew's and Luke's versions, including some scholarship on early African

---

[1] See the following useful references: Tommy Wasserman, "Manuscripts of the Lord's Prayer," *SBL*, at http://www.bibleodyssey.org/en/passages/related-articles/manuscripts-of-the-lords-prayer.aspx; C. Clifton Black, "The Lord's Prayer (Matt 6:9-13/Luke 11:2-4)," *SBL*, at http://www.bibleodyssey.org/passages/main-articles/lords-prayer.aspx.

engagements.[2] But the focus in this essay is on the economic "shape" of the prayer.[3]

Matthew's version is clearly about "economic matters."[4] Indeed, the Lord's Prayer is located within the extended covenantal renewal discourse that we know as the "Sermon on the Mount," in which "Jesus is delivering new covenantal teaching addressed to socio-economic interaction in small communities [...] demanding [...] rigorously disciplined justice in social-economic relations."[5] The Lord's Prayer takes up, in summary form, many of the covenantal demands of the Sermon on the Mount, placing in the mouths of Jesus' disciples a commitment to the economic dimensions of God's "new" covenant.

The economic elements are clear from the outset. There is a reference to "daily bread," a phrase that is unusual because the adjective "daily" is not used anywhere else in Greek literature. The phrase could be translated as "bread for today," or "bread for the following day," or "bread for the future," or "bread necessary for existence."[6] With each of these translations there is a recognition that for many who pray this prayer there will be a need for bread, for each day, day by day.

There is also the reference to "debts," a reference that is repeated in the reference to "debtors." This repetition, in such a short prayer, signals its importance. Debt, as we will discover, was a defining feature of the economic system of the ancient world.

So economic matters seem central to the prayer. What, if the whole prayer is a form of economic manifesto?

INSERTING A COLON

A colon as a form of punctuation is often used to signal an explanation or start an enumeration. We do not have any guide as the original punctuation of the Lord's Prayer, so each Bible translation has to determine how to

---

[2] Michael Joseph Brown, *The Lord's Prayer through North African Eyes: A Window into Early Christianity* (New York and London: T&T Clark, 2004).

[3] Luke's version of the prayer also retains a strong economic orientation, but the reference to "sin" rather than "debt" deflects our attention from the economic dimensions.

[4] For a general overview of the ancient economy in the time of Jesus, see David A. Fiensy, *Christian Origins and the Ancient Economy* (Cambridge: Lutterworth Press, 2014).

[5] Richard A. Horsley, *Covenant Economics: A Biblical Vision of Justice for All* (Louisville: Westminster John Knox Press, 2009), 153–54.

[6] Black, op. cit. (note 1).

punctuate the prayer. A colon is used after the first sentence: "Pray then in this way," indicating that what follows is the prayer that Jesus taught his disciples. But what, I want to ask, if we place another colon at the end of verse 10?

> [9]Pray then in this way: Our Father in heaven, hallowed be your name. [10]Your kingdom come. Your will be done, on earth as it is in heaven. [11]Give us this day our daily bread. [12]And forgive us our debts, as we also have forgiven our debtors. [13]And do not bring us to the time of trial, but rescue us from the evil one.

If we place a colon at the end of verse 10, we can then understand verses 11–13 as the explanation or enumeration of what Jesus means by "Your kingdom come. Your will be done, on earth as it is in heaven." But in order to understand the radical economic dimensions of my suggestion, we need first to pause and consider verse 10.

Most Christians do not believe verse 10. We do not believe that Jesus really asks us to pray for the kingdom of God to come "on earth." Most of us have been infected by forms of Christian theology that minimize this world and focus on the world to come, the world of heaven. But Jesus refutes this theology, making it clear that his disciples are to pray for God's kingdom to come and God's will to be done "on earth." Heaven is referred to, but only because it offers the model of what should come and be done "on earth." Earth is to be the destination of God's kingdom.

If we take verse 10 seriously then this requires a fundamental shift in much of our Christian theology, particularly the "evangelical" forms of Christian theology.[7] Our focus, according to this prayer, should be "on earth," with "as it is in heaven" providing the model, not the destination.

But what is the model being referred to by the phrase "as it is in heaven"? If we place a colon at the end of this phrase, at the end of verse 10 we are offered a summary of what Jesus anticipates by and includes in the phrase "as it is in heaven." Verses 11–13 provide the "shape" of God's economic hope for this world:

> Give us this day our daily bread. And forgive us our debts, as we also have forgiven our debtors. And do not bring us to the time of trial, but rescue us from the evil one.

---

[7] My reference to "evangelical" theology includes the older forms of Pentecostal and Charismatic Christianity. The newer forms of Pentecostal and Charismatic Christianity are more "this worldly," but in problematic ways, emphasizing as they do the individual, not the community or social systems; see, for example, Paul Gifford, *Ghana's New Christianity: Pentecostalism in a Globalizing African Economy* (Bloomington & Indianapolis: Indiana University Press, 2004).

My use of the term "shape" is significant. In the South African struggle against apartheid we emphasized the shape of the gospel.[8] The gospel, we argued, had a particular shape, it was "good news for the poor." So when Jesus addressed those gathered in the synagogue in his home town, Nazareth, he quoted from the law and the Prophets, using Scripture to provide the shape of his ministry: "'The Spirit of the Lord is upon me, because he has anointed me to bring good news to the poor'" (Lk 4:18). Again, I would argue that a colon would be appropriate at the end of this verse, so that verses 18b-19 are then an enumeration of particular examples of the basic shape, what it means "to bring good news to the poor." It means: "He has sent me to proclaim release to the captives and recovery of sight to the blind, to let the oppressed go free, to proclaim the year of the Lord's favor" (Lk 4:18b-19). The content of the gospel may vary from context to context, but the basic shape of the gospel must remain; the gospel must be some form of "good news to the poor." If what we proclaim is not good news for the poor, it is not the gospel.

The Lord's Prayer, I argue, has a distinct economic shape, and the shape is found in verses 11-13. But before we come to these overtly economic elements, it is important to recognize that the introductory elements are equally radical, framing what is to come.

ANOTHER KINGDOM

As I have already indicated, the opening of the Lord's Prayer makes it clear that the focus is "unmistakably"[9] on God's kingdom coming "on earth." The hallowing of God's name that precedes this earthly focus also has an earthly orientation.

> In the Israelite tradition ... God "hallows" or "sanctifies" God's name by delivering the people from foreign empires, inspiring them to observe the covenantal statutes and ordinances, and ensuring that they have sufficient food (Ezek 36:22-23).[10]

God's kingdom is unlike the empires that dominate their region and their history. Unlike these empires, God's "kingdom" is not based on an economy of extraction but on an economy of redistribution.

---

[8] Albert Nolan, *God in South Africa: The Challenge of the Gospel* (Cape Town: David Philip, 1988).

[9] Horsley, op. cit. (note 5), 150.

[10] Ibid., 155.

The emphasis in the Sermon on the Mount as a whole and in the Lord's Prayer in particular is on the (re)building of God's community, with "kingdom" language being appropriated to signal the socioeconomic intent of God's project on earth.[11] The Lord's Prayer is both about "God's new act of deliverance and the intensification of communal efforts at cooperation and mutual aid."[12]

> The petitions for daily bread and cancellation of debts in the Lord's Prayer are covenantal as well as economic (Lk 11:2-4; Mt 6:9-13). The cancellation of debts every seven years was one of the basic covenantal mechanisms to keep people economically viable on their ancestral land [...]. The underlying point of all the covenantal commandments and mechanisms was to enable people to have sufficient food day by day, year by year [...].[13]

BREAD FOR TODAY

The Lord's Prayer recognizes the need for bread for each day, a need that would have been a vital need for many of the economically marginalized of the first century. Jesus recognizes that many of those who follow him or listen to him are in need of bread for that day. This is why he is committed not only to teaching them but also to feeding them. When the disciples ask Jesus to dismiss the crowd he has been teaching, saying, "When it grew late, his disciples came to him and said, 'This is a deserted place, and the hour is now very late; send them away so that they may go into the surrounding country and villages and buy something for themselves to eat'" (Mk 6:35-36), Jesus rejects their suggestion, saying instead, "But he answered them, 'You give them something to eat'" (Mk 6:37).

So it is no accident that "bread" is such a common image in Jesus' teaching and ministry. Real bread is required by real people each day. And Jesus recognizes that many of those drawn to his project of community restoration[14] would not have the economic means to have bread each day.

---

[11] Joerg Rieger, *Christ and Empire: From Paul to Postcolonial Times* (Minneapolis: Fortress Press, 2007).

[12] Horsley, op. cit. (note 5), 112.

[13] Ibid., 99.

[14] See the following for reflection on the ministry of Jesus as being focused on the renewal or restoration of community: Richard A. Horsley, "The Kingdom of God and the Renewal of Israel," in Norman K. Gottwald and Richard A. Horsley (eds), *The Bible and Liberation: Political and Social Hermeneutics* (Maryknoll, NY.: Orbis, 1993), 408-27; Richard A. Horsley, "Moral Economy and Renewal Movement in Q," in Richard A. Horsley (ed.), *Oral Performance, Popular Tradition, and Hidden Tran-*

The first feature of the shape of Jesus' economic manifesto is the recognition that there are those who do not even have enough for each day. For the kingdom of God to come on earth, as it is in heaven, there must be bread each day for all. But Jesus does not stop here; charity is not enough. The economic systems that lead to people not having daily bread have to be addressed.

RELEASE FROM DEBT

The second feature of the shape of Jesus' economic manifesto is focused on the systemic dimensions of poverty. People are poor because of unjust and exploitative economic systems. This is the analysis of Jesus, for debt is the central mechanism of poverty in the world of his time. Indeed, debt is a central mechanism of ancient economies.[15] The rich are rich because the poor are poor. There is a causal, systemic relationship between those who are rich and those who are poor.[16] And debt is perhaps the most important of elements in the system.

The economic logic of debt is evident in one of the most important biblical texts about economic matters in the Bible, 1 Samuel 8:11-17.[17] The background to this text is the growing desire by the elders of ancient Israel for their "nation"' to be like other nations. In their words, they are concerned that the current decentralized economic and governance system was becoming corrupt (1 Sam 8:3) and so insist that they want "to have a king over us, so that we also may be like other nations, and that our king may govern us and go out before us and fight our battles" (1 Sam 8:19-20). Although the economic system of clan-based villages gave each family and clan access to and ownership of their own land and what it produced, the system of clan-based communities with clan-based judges did not offer a centralized system of monarchic government, with a centralized judicial system and a centralized military. The powerful city-temple states that surrounded ancient Israel, including those of Egypt, Assyria, and Philistia, all had centralized monarchic economic systems that supported centralized

---

script in *Q*, Semeia Studies (Atlanta: Society of Biblical Literature, 2006), 143-57; Horsley, op. cit. (note 5).

[15] Roland Boer, "The Sacred Economy of Ancient 'Israel'," in *Scandinavian Journal of the Old Testament: An International Journal of Nordic Theology* 21, no. 1 (2007), 29-48; Gerald O. West, "Tracking an Ancient near Eastern Economic System: The Tributary Mode of Production and the Temple-State," in *Old Testament Essays* 24, no. 2 (2011), 511-32.

[16] Gunther Wittenberg, *Resistance Theology in the Old Testament: Collected Essays* (Pietermaritzburg: Cluster Publications, 2007), 74-75.

[17] West, op. cit. (note 15), 514-15.

judicial and military systems. Forgetting that it was such systems that had enslaved their ancestors, the elders of Israel yearned to be like these nations.

Both Samuel the judge and Yahweh the God who heard the cry of slaves in Egypt (Ex 3:7) are dismayed by this request, and so Yahweh urges Samuel to "solemnly warn them [the elders of Israel], and show them the ways of the king who shall reign over them" (1 Sam 8:9). This Samuel does, stating:

> These will be the ways of the king who will reign over you: he will take your sons and appoint them to his chariots and to be his horsemen, and to run before his chariots; and he will appoint for himself commanders of thousands and commanders of fifties, and some to plow his ground and to reap his harvest, and to make his implements of war and the equipment of his chariots. He will take your daughters to be perfumers and cooks and bakers. He will take the best of your fields and vineyards and olive orchards and give them to his courtiers. He will take one-tenth of your grain and of your vineyards and give it to his officers and his courtiers. He will take your male and female slaves, and the best of your cattle and donkeys, and put them to his work. He will take one-tenth of your flocks, and you shall be his slaves (1 Sam 8:11–17).

The economic logic is clear. A monarchic city-temple state would require the villages' resources in order to establish and sustain a centralized judicial and military system. The king would "take." What is not stated, because it would have been apparent to the implied audiences of this text, is that the mechanism that links the king's taking and the people becoming slaves to the king is debt.

By having to offer tribute/taxation to the king in return for governance and military protection the ordinary villagers of early ancient Israel would have occasionally been forced to borrow. The kinds of tribute required by the monarchic city-temple state included human capacity, land and livestock and produce. The combination of having to pay tribute with a reduced labor force and reduced land holdings would force each family-clan to take loans in order to survive. When they were unable to repay the loans, indebtedness would result in forfeiting further land as surety. The compounding of debt led to a relentless process of the loss of land, tenant farming, day-laboring, and eventually debt-slavery.[18] The end result of the system over time was debt-slavery—being forced through debt to sell oneself in order to survive.

David and then Solomon implemented a tributary economic system, in which local villages were required to pay tribute in return for the governance

---

[18] This process is described vividly in Genesis 47:13–21, where Joseph implements a form of debt-slavery.

and protection of the city-state.[19] The impact of Solomon's extraction of trib-ute, particularly from the northern clans of Israel, was massive debt-slavery. And when Solomon died and the debt-enslaved peoples of Israel petitioned Solomon's son, Rehoboam, for respite, to which he responds: "My father made your yoke heavy, but I will add to your yoke; my father disciplined you with whips, but I will discipline you with scorpions" (1 Kings 12:14). The elders of Judah advise Rehoboam to heed the voice of the economically exploited work-ers (1 Kings 12:6-7), remembering perhaps their own history of enslavement. But Rehoboam ignores their advice, taking instead the advice of "the young men" (1 Kings 8-11), his city-based élite companions, who did not want to give up the luxuries that the forced labor of the northern clans provided. But the northern clans of Israel had had enough, and so they rebelled against Rehoboam and the house of David and Solomon, leading to an everlasting split between the northern clans and the southern clan of Judah.

The tributary economic system implemented by David and established by Solomon had become oppressive. And the core mechanism of oppression was debt. This was no accident. Debt was a key mechanism in the system of riches for a few and poverty for many.

The tributary economic system dominated the entire world of the Ancient Near East and endured into the time of Jesus. Empire after em-pire—whether Egyptian, Davidic, Assyrian, Babylonian, Persian, Hellenis-tic, or Roman—implemented the same system, building their empires on debt-slavery. By the time of Jesus the area of Palestine was full of tenant farmers, day-laborers, and debt-slaves. So it is not surprising that much of Jesus' teaching engages with this reality. The parable of the day-laborers who work for a few hours each day is a good example (Mt 20:1-16), though Matthew's framing of the parable reduces its economic impact.[20]

Another good example is the poor widow in Mark 12:41-44.[21] Jesus and his disciples watch as she puts her last few copper coins into the treasury. What we forget but what is clear in the biblical text is that in verse 40 Jesus had warned his disciples and the crowd who is listening to him that the temple scribes "devour widows' houses." The Jerusalem temple was a part of the tributary economic system, providing loans and expropriating land when the loans could not be repaid. And the system was administered in

---

[19] West, op. cit. (note 15), 516-20.

[20] William R. Herzog, *Parables as Subversive Speech: Jesus as Pedagogue of the Oppressed* (Louisville: Westminster/John Knox, 1994), 79-97; Gerald O. West and Sithembiso Zwane, ""Why Are You Sitting There?" Reading Matthew 20:1-16 in the Context of Casual Workers in Pietermaritzburg, South Africa," in Nicole Duran Wilkinson and James Grimshaw (eds), *Matthew: Texts @ Contexts* (Minneapolis: Fortress Press, 2013).

[21] West, op. cit. (note 15), 528-29.

part by the temple scribes. Either through debt or some related from of economic exploitation, the property of the widow here has been "devoured." Now she has little; and yet she still gives to the very system that has exploited her. The point Jesus makes, as he had said earlier, is: "Is it not written, 'My house shall be called a house of prayer for all the nations'? But you have made it a den of robbers" (Mk 11:17).

Understanding the damage done by debt-slavery[22] and being surrounded by the system's victims, Jesus teaches his disciples to pray that those who are indebted will be released from their debts: "And release us from our debts, as we also have released our debtors." By adding the second part of the sentence Jesus makes it clear that his disciples have to take the lead in releasing those indebted to them. They cannot expect to be released from their debts if they are not willing to release those indebted to them. Indeed,

> hallowing God's name points directly to the mutual forgiveness articulated in the petition to "release our debts, *as we herewith release those of our debtors.*" The exhortation to "forgive others" attached to the end of prayer (6:14-15) makes unmistakably clear that the cancellation of debts is the emphasis of the prayer in the covenantal speech in Matthew 5-7.[23]

Jesus here breaks the cycle of debt and so breaks the back of an economic system that enriches some but does so by enslaving many. The release of debt enables ordinary villagers to retain their land, enabling them to provide for their daily bread. By breaking the cycle of debt, the dignity, agency and capacity of ordinary village families was restored. No wonder that the early Jesus community "spread rapidly into rural areas near Galilee," having "taken hold in the lives of peasant producers whose religion was inseparable from their concern about debts and daily bread."[24]

THE TEMPTATIONS OF THE SYSTEM

The final sentence in the Lord's Prayer offers a warning: "And do not bring us to the time of trial, but rescue us from the evil one."[25] Resisting

---

[22] Douglas E. Oakman, *Jesus, Debt, and the Lord's Prayer: First-Century Debt and Jesus' Intentions* (Eugene: Cascade, 2014).
[23] Horsley, op. cit. (note 5), 155.
[24] Ibid., 112.
[25] The NRSV's translation "evil one" is a sign that this translation is unable to recognize the systemic dimensions of the Lord's Prayer. They have opted for a personal designation ("evil one").

exploitative economic systems is difficult because there are those of us who benefit from them. This is why so few white South Africans resisted the race-based economic system of apartheid. White South Africans benefited from apartheid. This is why so few in the so-called developed world resist globalized capitalism; many in the developed world benefit from it.

Jesus understands how easy it is to be coopted by oppressive economic systems, and so he warns his disciples not be tempted by unjust economic systems. Instead, he insists, we must recognize them for what they are—they are evil: "And do not lead us into temptation, but deliver us from evil."

Conclusion

As the church became more distant from the realities of the early Jesus movement and its commitment to social transformation, so the Lord's Prayer gradually lost its radical economic message. "Debt" became a metaphor for "sin." The Lord's Prayer became personal rather than communal, spiritual rather than social.

But the teaching of Jesus cannot be fully coopted, and so the subversive memory of an economic message remains forever in Matthew's version. Indeed, when we are overt about considering the economic message of Scripture we cannot but be confronted by the God who heeds the cry of slaves and constitutes them as the preferential people of God. We cannot but be confronted by the prophets who speak truth to the power of the monarchy. We cannot but be confronted by the Christ who comes to bring good news to the poor, and instructs that we pray as follows:

> Pray then in this way: Our Father in heaven, hallowed be your name. Your kingdom come. Your will be done, on earth as it is in heaven. Give us this day our daily bread. And forgive us our debts, as we also have forgiven our debtors. And do not bring us to the time of trial, but rescue us from the evil one.

Praying this version of the Lord's Prayer is a constant liturgical reminder of the economic shape of the gospel. Praying this version of the Lord's Prayer is a constant call to socioeconomic transformation in our globalized world.

"You cannot serve God and wealth"

Petri Merenlahti

In his Sermon on the Mount, Jesus said loudly and clearly:

> No one can serve two masters; for a slave will either hate the one and love the other, or be devoted to the one and despise the other. You cannot serve God and wealth (Mt 6:24).

What exactly did Jesus mean? What should and do his words mean today, taking into account that today's Christians are a patchwork of different people, living in different contexts and under different circumstances? What does it mean, here and now, not to serve mammon but to serve the living God?

What kind of an economist was Jesus?

Jesus preached radical economic freedom, but not in the classical liberal sense. He did not preach freedom to grab whatever one likes and to make it one's own. Rather, he preached freedom from worry and lack; freedom to benefit from mutual care; freedom not to be ruled by greed, fear, loneliness, or poverty, but to have life in abundance.

Unlike John the Baptist, Jesus was not an austere ascetic but, rather, a happy consumer—even to the point that people took offence (cf. Mt 11:18–19). It is not food or drink or merry company but selfishness that should be given up. Everyone should have equal access to the good things in life.

That is why Jesus says we must free ourselves from mammon as well as the wrong priorities, false security and economic oppression that slavery to mammon entails. We cannot base our livelihood on greed, because individual greed will make others poor and lead to loneliness. We cannot base security on fear, because no wall will be high enough to protect us from the suspicion and bitterness that walls provoke among people. And we cannot create human value by taking advantage of our fellow human beings, since that would be an offence, not just against their human dignity but also against our own.

Therefore, besides freeing ourselves from slavery to greed, we must also free ourselves from hunger for power in order not to exploit other people and use them for our private gain. Indeed, there is no legitimate authority except for the common good. God did not create a humanity of masters and slaves but a humanity of God's children—all equal and all of equal worth. Therefore, the sole duty of any rightful authority is to serve the common humanity, which is why whoever wants to be first must be the last of all and servant of all, just as Jesus came not to be served but to serve (cf. Mk 10:44–45). Service, and only that, is what power is for.

Moreover, we must free ourselves from fear and worry and from the false belief that we need mammon and power in order to be safe. As Jesus said to his disciples,

> Therefore I tell you, do not worry about your life, what you will eat, or about your body, what you will wear. For life is more than food, and the body more than clothing. [...] Instead, strive for [God's] kingdom, and these things will be given to you as well. [...] Sell your possessions, and give alms. Make purses for yourselves that do not wear out, an unfailing treasure in heaven, where no thief comes near and no moth destroys. For where your treasure is, there your heart will be also (Lk 12:22–23, 31, 33–34).

"There your heart will be also." This is the key to Jesus' economic theory. It is an economy of the heart. For while our bodies need food and shelter and health, what we really benefit from in our God-given life are the things we keep in our hearts: the people we love; the values we hold dear; the faith we keep; and the principles we hold onto. Money can buy none of these; none of them should be for sale. Therefore, whatever we do with money in our societies, we should make sure it is money that serves the people, and not the other way round. In other words, we should not let money into our hearts. Our hearts belong to someone else.

"Make purses for yourselves that do not wear out." The true benefit humanity can reap from the business of life lies in the opportunities that we have to participate in the circulation of love, justice and God's grace—this is where humanity should invest its money, time and entire being. In the words of the prophet Isaiah, we are called "to lose the bonds of injustice, to undo the thongs of the yoke, to let the oppressed go free, and to break every yoke"; "to share our bread with the hungry, and bring the homeless poor into our house; when we see the naked, to cover them, and not to hide ourselves from our own kin" (Isa 58:6–7) These are the kind of shares we should have in our portfolios, as they will bring forth grain, thirty, sixty, a hundredfold (Mt 13:8). They are the kind of business opportunities we should not miss—for what will it profit us if we gain the whole world but forfeit our lives? (cf. Mt 16:26)

Indeed we should go and learn from the shrewd managers of our age, so as to seize every opportunity to capitalize on our assets of faith, hope and love (cf. Lk 16:1–13). "You received without payment," says Jesus, so "give without payment" (Mt 10:8). "Give to everyone who begs from you; and if anyone takes away your goods, do not ask for them again. Do to others as you would have them do to you" (Lk 6:30–31).

This is not a personal charity program but the foundation of a whole new community with an entirely new economic order—the body of Christ.

WHAT KIND OF AN ECONOMY IS THE BODY OF CHRIST?

Jesus' followers were a movement that requires of us that we get our priorities right: for the sake of God and our fellow human beings, our values, relationships and future need to be put before greed, cynicism and fear. Do this, and you will have life in abundance. Do this, and you will not be alone. Even God's spirit will come to help you.

Those who took heed formed a radical spiritual community, a common economy of mutual sharing. St Luke described it in Acts: "All who believed were together," he wrote, "and had all things in common; they would sell their possessions and goods and distribute the proceeds to all, as any had need" (Acts 2:44–45).

The apostolic community was a welfare economy, united by a sense of belonging. This was captured by the community's new and energetic international missions manager, St Paul of Tarsus, who introduced the image of the church as the body of Christ. As one body, all the church's gains and losses inevitably were collective: "If one member suffers, all suffer together with it; if one member is honored, all rejoice together with it" (1 Cor 12:26).

Therefore, in the body of Christ, God is truly incarnate in the common good of God's people, making inclusive care not only a moral but religious obligation. St James writes,

> If a brother or sister is naked and lacks daily food and one of you says to them, "Go in peace; keep warm and eat your fill," and yet you do not supply their bodily needs, what is the good of that? So faith by itself, if it has no works, is dead (Jas 2:15–17).

Likewise, St John: "How does God's love abide in anyone who has the world's goods and sees a brother or sister in need and yet refuses help?" (1 Jn 3:17).

As a welfare economy, the body of Christ is an economy of equals. The way of the world may be to pay special respect to the noble and the rich and the powerful, but God sees people differently. God created everyone, God loves everyone, God welcomes everyone. Therefore, as St Paul said, "there is no longer Jew or Greek, there is no longer slave or free, there is no longer male and female; for all of you are one in Christ Jesus" (Gal 3:28).

The body of Christ is a global welfare economy based on equal participation: everyone is included. God hears the cries of all those who suffer, and therefore the body of Christ, the community in which God became flesh, must hear the cries of all those who suffer. Therefore every ecclesiastical body needs a constitution that ensures that all its members will be heard and their needs addressed. In addition, every church, congregation and ministry needs a strong operational arm for delivering humanitarian aid and advocating for social justice.

The love of God is, and the love of the body of Christ incarnate must be, universal. It includes the widow and the orphan—those who are the most vulnerable in our societies. It includes the stranger—those who we do not readily think of as "us" and who are therefore at constant risk of discrimination. It even includes the enemy—those who we think wish us no good and as such are the most vulnerable of all, if they ever end up being at our mercy. They all are God's children and we must treat them accordingly. For like Jesus said, "[God] makes his sun rise on the evil and on the good, and sends rain on the righteous and on the unrighteous" (Mt 5:45).

This is indeed a radical spiritual, social and economic program, if there ever was one. One might even call it revolutionary. Yet, it is to come into the world in a peaceful way. Christians are not forcibly to apply the rule of God over anyone, but to lead by example, voluntarily. Meanwhile, as Paul suggests to his fellow Christians in Rome, they will "pay to all what is due them—taxes to whom taxes are due, revenue to whom revenue is due, respect to whom respect is due, honor to whom honor is due" (Rom 13:7).

While voluntary, it is essential that a Christian economic order is systemic and has a long-term focus. Justice is key for the common good of any community and the best possible protection the most vulnerable can hope for is that everyone's human rights be respected. After all, anyone of us may one day end up being in the most vulnerable position; vulnerability is one of the few things that are truly universally human. We all get hurt; we all make mistakes; we may all fall ill; we all have to die. So it is not merely some abstract, remote others, such as the blessed poor in the slums and refugee camps, who need protection and be given the possibility to live their lives in dignity. They do, because we all do, every day. We all are one. In Christ.

What kind of an economy is the body of Christ? In brief, it is an economy of hospitality that seeks to replace greed, fear and cynicism with universal care, universal rights and universal participation. It is an economy based on miracles and capable of miracles. It is an economy that heals the sick and teaches wisdom to children. It is an economy of abundant life for all people and the entire creation. It is an economy in which spiritual, social and economic welfare all meet and become one.

Is it a possible economy? Is it possible today? Is it possible where we come from, you and me? What would it take to make it grow? That, I guess, would be God's question to us today.

WHY WITH IMPATIENCE DO I PRAY?
JUSTIFICATION AND JUSTICE:
THE CRY OF THE LAND AND THE PEOPLE

Nancy Cardoso

> Then Jesus told them a parable about their need to pray always and not to lose heart. He said, "In a certain city there was a judge who neither feared God nor had respect for people. In that city there was a widow who kept coming to him and saying, "Grant me justice against my opponent." For a while he refused; but later he said to himself, "Though I have no fear of God and no respect for anyone, yet because this widow keeps bothering me, I will grant her justice, so that she may not wear me out by continually coming." And the Lord said, "Listen to what the unjust judge says. And will not God grant justice to his chosen ones who cry to him day and night? Will he delay long in helping them? I tell you, he will quickly grant justice to them. And yet, when the Son of Man comes, will he find faith on earth?" (Lk 18:1-8).

Imagine the woman in Luke 18. She is on her way to meet the judge. She is a widow without rights and he, a powerful man, an authority. He is a judge. He does not recognize anyone or anything in the heavens above or down here on earth, among the people.

Imagine her with sweaty hands and trembling knees. Humble, perhaps, determined, certainly. He, the judge, is proud of himself and has no time for crying and grumbling. He thinks that he has control over the system. But he does not. She has the dignity of the poor, the powerless, the weak ones—that is her strength.

She is persistent and motivated in her struggle while she is on her way to meet an indifferent judge. She has nothing, but each step on the way is an experience of learning and empowerment.

He will say no. He will not listen to her. He will turn his back on her. He will humiliate her with his silence, his aggressiveness and his strategy always to postpone solutions that would help people in need with the help of the law. And she will persist. She will keep going, moving from her non-existence to the affirmation of her life and dignity. Look at her. Look at the thousands of women with no access to clean water and affordable and adequate health care. Was your mother treated like this? Was she treated with disdain and humiliated? Do you know people who, every day, have to struggle against unfair conditions—the lack of basic necessities, food, education and health care. The class struggle continues daily and new forms of exclusion, racism and sexism emerge.

Today and tomorrow, she will come. She organizes herself with others; she is a multitude, she is a movement. She has nothing—but she has everything to share. She has hope—the hope to keep going.

As we read in Luke 18 she is so persistent that the judge is afraid of her. And Jesus said, this is how you have to pray!

She is the migrant on a boat adrift on the ocean: look at her! She is the young Palestinian woman just minutes before being killed at a checkpoint in Hebron: look at her! She is the desperate mother of a young black man killed by police in São Paulo: look at her! She is the farmer in an African country threatened by mining: look at her! She is the foreign worker who cleans the ground you walk on in the USA: look at her! She is the indigenous woman fighting against an oil company: look at her! She is the feminist peasant who fights for land and bread: look at her! And do not tell them how they should suffer, how they should live, or how they should fight. With them we learn to pray.

THE WHEEL IS BROKEN.

"CHANGING THE WHEEL"

I sit by the roadside
The driver changes the wheel.
I do not like the place I have come from.
I do not like the place I am going to.
Why with impatience do I
Watch him changing the wheel? (Bertolt Brecht)[1]

---

[1] http://kingsreview.co.uk/articles/changing-the-wheel-bertolt-brechts-stories-from-the-revolution/

According to the Map of Inequality, in 2013, the richest ten percent of the planet owned eighty-six percent of the global wealth. Of these, 0.7 percent possessed USD 98.7 trillion –the largest amount recorded in human history.

Hegemonic power structures such as capitalism, militarism, racism and patriarchy impact our life on planet earth. While they are often protected by media that help to mask their influence, the threat is nonetheless real, affecting people and whole regions in terms of inequality and systemic violence and enabling access to resources only to some. Dissidents and those who resist are criminalized. All of humanity is affected by greed and the scourge of capitalism. The global élite, those who are in control and have the power to decide and act, are at best interested in mitigating the impact and not in changing structures. They change the wheel, manage the crisis they have created in order to protect their interests—the accumulation of capital—regardless of what it takes and regardless of how many wars they have to fight in order to achieve this.

The wheel is broken! Capitalism is not working!

The relentless wheel of capitalism destroys local economies, ancestral ways of life and democratic alternatives to the way in which life is organized. Crises upon crises justify economic adjustments that save capitalism and eternally plunge people, countries, communities and the future into debt, leading to poverty, destruction and indignity.

> But we ask you:
> Even if it's not very strange, find it estranging
> Even if it is usual, find it hard to explain
> What here is common should astonish you
> What here's the rule, recognize as an abuse
> And where you have recognized an abuse
> Provide a remedy.[2]

What is needed is to see the world differently, to think and to organize life in community in alternative ways. Totally immersed in the "undignified" logic of the broken wheel that is being renewed time and again, we

---

[2] Bertolt Brecht, *The Exception and the Rule,* at https://books.google.ch/books?id=mXMMYengvkcC&printsec=frontcover&dq=Brecht+The+exception+and+the+rule&hl=en&sa=X&ved=0ahUKEwiksrrj-ODUAhVJsxQKHdKEC4sQ6AEILzAD#v=onepage&q=%20The%20exception%20and%20the%20rule&f=false .

limit ourselves by trying to defend fragments of life. All our prayers, our searching for joy are crushed by the suffering of humanity and the world.

Spirituality is diminished and religion itself reduced to defending private life and one's possessions and salvation postponed in rituals to survive. We pray, "Forgive us our debts as we forgive our debtors," unaware that this way we denounce the toothed wheel of capitalism and its eternal debts and announce forgiveness as the creation of life—enhancing space where shared power relationships and reciprocity deliver liberating and creative tools for other ways of humbly walking with God in the world and of being human in a dignified way.

THE DRIVER CHANGES THE WHEEL

Who is the one changing the wheel? The one who is driving? It is the owner of the car and the wheel and, obviously, this is the one who has the authority to change the broken wheel.

Throughout history, the "owners" and "drivers" have repeatedly been called upon to solve the crisis of poverty and destruction. The "drivers" recognize themselves in the other without posing hard questions pertaining to legitimacy, democracy and justice.

Governments and politicians, technology companies and data management companies, churches and church agencies are called upon to be protagonists in the fight against poverty. As Albert Einstein said, "a new type of thinking is essential if [hu]mankind is to survive and move to higher levels".[3]

According to the Map of Inequality at least half of humanity is paralyzed, sitting at the margins—the margins of the big discussion forums. "We should include ..." say churches and their agencies!

The urgency of the task, namely to end poverty and protect the planet, cannot be solved with the same logic that promotes and perpetuates the problems, and not even by the same "drivers."

Dignity should not only be a goal, it should be a way of moving forward. Dignifying those whose voices have been marginalized implies the radical socialization of mechanisms of discussion, resolution and the implementation of decisions and policies. This means to acknowledge that there are diverse and divergent "knowledges" that can contribute as protagonists to the agenda itself, to its priorities and goals, and not just be subsequently included.

We have to take a side! Or, are we still patient with this broken wheel? Do we still accept the leadership of the agents of governments and capitalists and remain seated by the road?

---

[3] In the interview by Michael Amrine titled, "The Real Problem is in the Hearts of Men," *New York Times Magazine* (23 June 1946).

The dignity of the world and its beings can only be defended with the dignity of the world and its beings. Technological innovations, data management and governances need to be a part of the effort for dignity and not the effort itself. In order to reach this aim, new and collective democratic control, what we call the radicalization of democracy, is vital. To go on with the same wheel of the same car and the same drivers means to continue to drag the world and its beings into barbarism and to deny dignity.

"Let us not fall into temptation, but deliver us from evil," we pray with conviction but we easily allow ourselves to be won over and coopted by the responses of the powerful voices that promise us objectivity, scientific knowledge and political effectiveness.

No! Deliver us from evil!

Luther's teaching on justification by grace through faith in Christ alone (Rom 5:1) is a legitimate and liberating interpretation of Scripture that emerged in the context of the oppressions of late medieval piety and against an emergent money lending-for-interest economy. Forgiveness of sins by grace, deliverance from the power of the devil, and the promise of eternal life in this context meant not only spiritual freedom but freedom for reconciliation with and ethical responsibility for the neighbor.[4]

While for Luther justification by grace alone expressed this understanding of equality, the Reformation failed to concretize it in social and economic terms. In fact, later Lutheranism even turned social and economic inequality into a hierarchical God-given order! This culminated in asserting the autonomy of the market and/or the state, which both Scripture and Luther explicitly critique.

A dignified spirituality is needed for the task before us, namely to rethink existing power structures. In order to make the radical changes needed we need to recognize people's organizations and social movements as the ones with the ability and legitimacy to take control of the car and to make the necessary changes.

I do not like the place I come from
—I do not like the place I am going to

Look at the scenarios that have brought us to this point—the exhaustion of the planet and the indignity of the human experience. What would be

---

[4] Martin Luther, "The Freedom of a Christian (1520)", in *LW 31*, 329-77.

"prosperity/progress" understood as the development of a "strong, inclusive and transformative" economy that is guided by growth? Whose growth?

The promise that a strong economy leads us to shared prosperity is never fulfilled because the conditions for strength and growth always prioritize the reproduction of the economic system and the time for sharing never comes. The defense of "strength and growth" justifies the reduction of the "wealth of natural resources" to merchandise. Nature is neither a "wealth of resources" nor an "economic opportunity." The need for endless growth of capital expresses itself in the exploitation of labor and nature.

The place we come from pushes us onto the verge of a crisis of civilization. I do not like the place I come from nor the place I am going to, or, rather, where the powerful ones are trying to take us either by trying to convince us or by repression and war.

We want another world! Don't ask me to accept what you consider "possible"! What social movements and organized communities are struggling for is an "another way to organize life."

"Give us this day our daily bread," we pray. Finding new ways of organizing life challenges the entire logic of consumerism, accumulation and excess that define the ways of living in the market and regulate society. The "bread" is "ours"—this little phrase expresses dignity! The "bread" as something that is at the same time the result of human work and God's creation, a symbol for our relation with nature and with culture ... it is ours! Collective and plural. And the "bread is ours" "every day" and "today."

And so—for the "bread" to be "ours" and to be "daily" we are called to walk at a slower pace, to decrease our footprints in the world.

The "every day" needs to motivate us to undo development and to remake the world (Ivan Illich). Cultivate seeds of de-growth, of *Sumak Kawsay*, of *bien vivir*, not in order to seek negative growth rates or to immobilize science, but to remake the way to innovating and planning as a "slow science": "Slow science" claims less haste and greater popular participation in decision making about which scientific experiments should be carried forward, through greater general awareness of the risks and benefits of each one of them.

WHY DO I IMPATIENTLY WATCH THEM CHANGING THE WHEEL?

On the path to "dignity" we already live now as we want to live tomorrow. Combatting poverty is done with the participation of the poor; respect for the planet is not just a remote goal but we respect it already now, without steps and without agreements that delay the present on behalf of a conditioned future.

We need to balance on the tight rope of social and planetary revolution, patience and impatience. To encourage the new implies seeing it where it is already now and give meaning beyond instrumental reason; being able to create the possibilities for understanding the ongoing new requirements, which is not only defined by the "innovation of the new" but also the "innovation of the old", i.e., the reconfiguration of the "knowledges" of the poor of the land, belittled until now, and new "knowledges" of the land itself, the planet and its grammar.

Sumak Kawsay is our heritage and promise: our never unlearned words. *Bien Vivir* as the connection to the past of the native peoples, how we want to live in community: eco-dependent, eco-socialists, eco-feminists being some of our most cherished words. These and other words that we collect, polish and exchange among ourselves as a necessary learning and an exercise of power sharing. *Kawsay sumak, suma qamaña, quilombos* or "land without evil" are not just concepts; they are names of the fighting events and utopia of indigenous peoples in Latin America, reference and motivation in popular struggles of the continent.

This spirituality of impatience and patience provides the ability to criticize, it hastens to deconstruct and leisurely creates the modes of redoing. The pace of everyday life thus provides a balanced way to organize, plan and carry out our engagement: linked to the world of needs and reproduction this approach becomes vital to the treatment of our common house: *oikos*!

Our "common house" is the expression of the spirituality and collective will to undo the node of capitalism and its toothed wheel, create defense mechanisms and be able to let the planet live without the pressure of "time for profit." In the lives of the people of and on the land the alternatives and possibilities are offered as exercises of the *bien vivir* already present among us. Dignity is already among us!

This is the time for dignity, which is also expressed in the commitments of those who live the faith in the gospel of Jesus:

- Denounce the historical and current relations of hegemonic Christianity with capitalism

- Promote a spiritual and cultural rejection of capitalism as a condition so that Christianity can be a part of the process to overcome poverty and to lift up the dignity of life

- Denounce Christianity trapped by the interests of the global élites in exchange for favors that support the accumulation and concentration of wealth, which legitimize the systematic forms of exploitation of human labor and nature

- Disown and denounce all worship of capital and the pseudo-religion of consumerism

- Deny the use of the Christian faith and the Bible as a justification for war, for the destruction of other religions and ways of life

- Affirm Christianity as a religion among others, as people of faith among other peoples of faith and call all Christians to fight for justice, to love mercy and to walk humbly with their God (Mic 6:8).

THEOLOGY AND LIFE IN ABUNDANCE

"WHAT ARE HUMAN BEINGS THAT YOU ARE MINDFUL OF THEM?": BEING HUMAN BEFORE GOD AND ONE ANOTHER IN PSALM 8, IN THE LUTHERAN TRADITION AND TODAY

Kenneth Mtata

CONTESTED EXISTENCE

To be regarded as a full human being is not self-evident; it is the result of competing, often conflicting perspectives on what constitutes a human being. In these struggles, power and interests play a crucial role, as well as ideologies, sometimes supported by pseudo-scientific research.

An example of such conflicting views in regard to human dignity can be brought from the times of the slave trade. On the one hand the slave trade offered economic benefits while, on the other, it troubled the conscience of some of those influenced by the Enlightenment vision of the dignity of all human beings. At the center of this tension was the perennial question: who "should be counted as human?"[1] To pacify their conscience, some slave owners had to "deny that African slaves were human."[2]

The dehumanization of European Jewry by the Nazis made it easier even for ordinary Germans to kill and carry out the Holocaust. The question what does or does not constitute the human being does not only play itself out in the mind,

---

[1] David Livingstone Smith, *Less than Human: Why we Demean, Enslave, and Exterminate Others* (New York: St Martin's Press, 2011), 1.
[2] Ibid.

but finds expression in the language used. What constitutes a human being is closely linked to language and imagery. In other words, anthropologies of life can be distinguished from anthropologies of death through language games as was clearly demonstrated in the 1994 Rwanda genocide. Tensions had been simmering since the 1959 Hutu uprising. But what fuelled the genocide was the description in the magazine, *Kangura* (Awaken!), of Tutsi people as "vile, sub-human creatures." "[A] cockroach cannot give birth to a butterfly. It is true. A cockroach gives birth to another cockroach... ." This description of the Tutsis as *inyenzi* (cockroaches) in the state propaganda, robbed them of their humanity and as such they could be eliminated without any troubled conscience.[3] It has been observed that in

> the midst of genocide, it becomes difficult to see any purely language-language moves concerning identity terms because everything becomes charged with actions, either getting into the game, or exiting it with non-discursive actions. "There are cockroaches at Nyange Church" said over the radio sounds like an observation, so seems like a language-entry move. But it gets messy once you understand the modes of indirection at work in the actual genocidal language games, which turned it into a (not very) oblique imperative to go kill the people in the church.[4]

The names ascribed to people can, in certain circumstances, shift their status from being human to being sub-human.

The above are examples of dehumanization. Similarly there are many examples of humanization, where individuals or groups vigorously fought with powerful ideas and actions, even embodying the struggle in how they organize institutions to ensure that others retain their humanity. But we have seen the exaltation of human majesty to the point of idolatry.

This paper identifies three main possible anthropologies, two of which are considered unhealthy. The first one is demonstrated by the examples above, where some are stripped of their humanity through the way in which they are (a) represented in language; (b) deprived of privileges in their daily lives; and (c) in the way in which society, institutions or organizations are systematically skewed against them. The second is one where a few are ascribed super-human recognition that exalts them to the level of semi-gods. The third is the healthy one that recognizes that all human beings are endowed with "glory and honor," (Ps 8:5). This view does not underestimate the potential frailty and vulnerability of all human beings, hence necessitating the need for constant struggle for the dignity of all.

---

[3] Ibid., 152

[4] Lynne Tirrell, "Studying Genocide: A Pragmatist Approach to Action-Engendering Discourse," in Graham Hubbs and Douglas Lind, *Pragmatism, Law, and Language* (New York: Routledge, 2014), 152–72, here 165.

The centrality of anthropology for theology and the other way round

If anthropology is a contest between different understandings of who is human with implications for life and death, we have no choice but to enter this battle. The early Christian writer describes this battle, "For our struggle is not against enemies of blood and flesh, but against the rulers (τὰς ἀρχάς), against the authorities (τὰς ἐξουσίας), against the cosmic powers (τοὺς κοσμοκράτορας) of this present darkness, against the spiritual forces of evil (πνευματικὰ τῆς πονηρίας) in the heavenly places" (Eph 6:12). If anthropologies can have destructive and liberating effects, it is vital that we find some clarity on what it means to be human in the context of doing theology, knowing that such a search is riddled with many challenges.

The first set of challenges has to do with the essence of being human: Is being human something inert, permanent, unalterable and eternal—something essential? Is the human being only a body? Or are there other non-material aspects to being human? If the human being's body is nurtured through physical food, what kind of food nurtures the non-material aspect of being human?

The second set of questions is epistemological; what is the appropriate source of knowledge about humans? Do we acquire the right knowledge about human beings from some objective study of their physical, psychological, sociological or any other form of makeup, or do we simply learn about being human beings from subjective and lived experiences? Are these lived experiences individual or aggregated? How do we know about the non-material side of the human person?

The third set of questions can be considered as ethical questions: Are human beings inherently good or bad or do they learn to be good or bad as they are being socialized? Why do people who have been socialized in the same way end up being so different? What is good or bad and why do people not always agree on this? Would human beings be able to do good if they agreed on what it is?

The fourth set of questions has to do with meaning: Why are we here as individuals and collectives? Is there some purpose to life? How can such meaningful living be lost or nurtured? How can the meaning and purpose of life be restored to those who have lost it?

A healthy anthropology for our time is a measured understanding of the human person with their majesty and honor on the one hand and vulnerability and frailty on the other. In the following, I shall draw on Psalm 8 and on Lutheran writings and will conclude by pointing to the implications of such an anthropology for the renewal of the church and society in our time.

THE HUMAN BEING IN PSALM 8

The whole Psalter is a book that reflects on the human being as one who stands before God and other creatures as both vulnerable and frail but also as majestic and honored. How the Psalms facilitate such an understanding of the self and of God was well captured by Martin Luther when he said:

> The heart of man[5] is a vessel on a lone sea, agitated by the tempest. At one time, fear and the anxiety of the future urge him on; at another, disappointment and present evils afflict him. Sometimes hope, or the desire of future good, excites him; and sometimes he is agitated by the joys of this present world. All these emotions are a great lesson for man: they teach him to cast anchor on firm word, and to steer out of this life towards a land of safety. In this tempestuous sea, what pilot better than the psalmist? Where else can he find language more consoling than in these canticles, which express praise and gratitude? [...] Whenever the psalmist wishes to express fear or hope, no painter's pencil can impart more brilliant colors; and Cicero would envy his treasures of imagery and eloquence. If you wish to see the Christian church arrayed in all the pomp and majesty, although narrowed in a small compass, take and read the psalms, and you will find the faithful mirror of Christianity. If you want to know yourself, God and his creatures, recur to the psalmist. [6]

Since we want to know ourselves and God and other creatures, we go back to the Psalms. In terms of the genre, Psalm 8 is identified as a praise psalm fulfilling the promise of the last verse of Psalm 7 "I will give to the Lord the thanks due to his righteousness, and sing praise to the name of the Lord, the Most High" (Ps 7:17).[7] Its overall thematic focus is praise to God's work "in creating the universe, and contrasts his unfathomable potency with man's diminished status in the grand scheme of created entities."[8] It is indeed the embodiment of worship since only in this psalm God is directly addressed in the second person. But it has also been rightly identified as a wisdom psalm since it "reflects on human nature in its two aspects, human frailty and mortality on the one hand and, on the other, the high status

---

[5] Please note that many of the quotations used do not use the gender sensitive language about collective humanity or about God. For the sake of the flow of the text I have not corrected this but I should highlight this as one challenge of language in shaping what it means to be human.

[6] *LW* 35, 256ff.

[7] Walter Brueggemann and William H. Bellinger, Jr., *Psalms* (New York: Cambridge University Press, 2014), 58.

[8] David Emanuel, "Matthew 21:16: 'From the Lips of Infants and Babes'—The Interpretation of Psalm 8:2 in Matt 21:16," in R. Steven Notley and Jeffrey P. Garcia (eds), *The Gospels in First-Century Judea* (Leiden: Brill, 2015), 47.

that has been granted to human beings (v. 6) together with dominion over all other created beings (vv. 7-9)."[9]

I propose a reading of Psalm 8 from its anthropological axis of verse 4: "What are human beings that you are mindful of them, mortals that you care for them?" This has been identified as the "swing verse" which provides the "ontological question."[10] This structure would use a division starting with the (a) editorial superscription; (b) followed by the prelude (v. 1a); (c) reference to the greatness of Yahweh (vv. 1b-2); (d) and the transitional question regarding the human being (vv. 3-4). After the transitional question, there is (e) an affirmation of the majesty of the human being (vv. 5-8) before closing with the postlude (vv. 9) as follows:

Superscript:
To the choirmaster. On the gittith. Psalm of David

Inclusio/refrain: Prelude: v. 1a
O Lord, our Sovereign, how majestic is your name in all the earth!

Strophe 1: The greatness of Yahweh: vv.1b-2
You have set your glory above the heavens. Out of the mouths of babes and infants you have founded a bulwark because of your foes, to silence the enemy and the avenger.

Strophe 2: The fragility of humanity: vv. 3-4
When I look at your heavens, the work of your fingers, the moon and the stars that you have established; what are human beings that you are mindful of them, mortals that you care for them?

Strophe 3: The greatness of humanity: vv. 5-8
Yet you have made them a little lower than God, and crowned them with glory and honor. You have given them dominion over the works of your hands; you have put all things under their feet, all sheep and oxen, and also the beasts of the field, the birds of the air, and the fish of the sea, whatever passes along the paths of the seas.

Inclusio/refrain: Postlude: v. 9
O Lord, our Sovereign, how majestic is your name in all the earth!

---

[9] Norman Whybray, *Reading the Psalms as a Book* (Sheffield: Sheffield Academic Press, 1996), 60.
[10] Clarence Hassel Bullock, *Psalms*: Volume 1: Psalms 1-72 (Grand Rapids: Baker Books, 2015).

My assumption here is that in its final form the Psalm, which begins with a superscription that alludes to its Davidic origin, may have been used in the context of worship if the obscure '"gittith" refers to some "melody, instrument, or proprietor of the Psalm."[11] But this worship could have been informed by the bewildering experience of the singer who sees the frailty and vulnerability of the human being in the face of a mighty God who has created the universe. And yet, this apparent insignificant being has been endowed with so much power, only slightly below the divine. Below I want to focus on the chiasmic arrangement of the prelude together with the postlude as providing the hermeneutical key to Psalm 8. I shall then look at the reference to the greatness of Yahweh. The next focus will be on the transitional question regarding the human being, before concluding with the affirmation of the majesty of human being.

PRELUDE

Although scholars do not agree on the details of the structure and the arrangement of stanzas of Psalm 8, they are in agreement that the body of the main material of the song is framed within a prelude (v. 2ab) and a similar postlude (v. 9).[12] The prelude and postlude form the chiasm that highlights the main theme of Psalm 8. Some scholars think that this theme is "a symphony of the delight upon the unfolding of the theology of the name,"[13] while others believe that the theme is "without a doubt creation, but secondary theme within the poem is royalty."[14] I think there could be several themes. The emphasis of one such theme is to highlight the relational anthropology, before God and creation.

The common line between the prelude and the postlude is: "O Lord, our Sovereign, how majestic is your name in all the earth!" (vv. 1b and 9). This expression is different from other psalms as it begins with praise itself instead of an invitation to worship. The worshipper identifies Yahweh as God (Yahweh) but also his Lord (Adonai). The worshipper stands before Yahweh whose name covers the whole earth. In the Old and New Testaments, the name of the Lord is closely linked to the presence of Yahweh[15] or the place where Yahweh chooses "self-disclosure."[16]

---

[11] Erhard Gerstenberger, *Psalm: Part 1: With an Introduction to Cultic Poetry* (Grand Rapids: Wm. B. Eerdmans, 1988), 67.

[12] Nancy L. deClaissé-Walford, Rolf A. Jacobson and Beth LaNeel Tanner (eds), *The Book of Psalms* (Grand Rapids: Wm. B. Eerdmans, 2014), 120.

[13] Ibid., 126.

[14] Ibid., 120.

[15] Sandra L. Richter, *The Deutronomistic History and the Name Theology* (Berlin: Walter de Gruyter, 2002), 11.

[16] Geoffrey Grogan, *Psalms* (Cambridge: Wm. B. Eerdmans, 2008), 302.

Here, the name of Yahweh is not confined to one place such as the Jerusalem temple. One can sense here an affirmation of one of the theological traditions regarding Yahweh's presence—one in which the divine presence is decentralized. In over sixty psalms worshippers are invited to sing praises to the name,[17] call on the name, praise the name, exalt the name, give thanks to the name, announce the name, fear the name, know the name, be saved by the name, love the name, not to forget the name and to seek the name.[18] Proverbs 18:10 points to the security of the name: "The name of the Lord is a strong tower; the righteous run into it and are safe".

The initial disclosure of the name was to Moses at Mount Sinai during God's liberation of the Israelites from the slavery of Egypt. Through this self-disclosure, Yahweh promises that "I will be what I will be" and the Israelites will be transformed from being slaves (not a people) into being a nation (a people). This name of Yahweh is transferable or, rather, shared with humans in a transformative way—those called by Yahweh's name become subjects of salvation as well as agents of redemption.

There was such closeness to authority and power of those angelic figures bearing the name of Yahweh that in rabbinic literature this was corrected as it threatened Yahweh's monotheism. This was especially true of angelic figures sent out by God to save God's people. This is prominent in the early Jewish Mystical tradition, on which basis the concept of the "son of man" as reference of Jesus in the New Testament can be understood. This "son of man" therefore performs a function akin to that of the angel who led Israelites out of Egypt."[19] Jonathan Draper has convincingly demonstrated how the coming of Jesus, especially as depicted in the Gospel of John, was interpreted from the same theological tradition where Jesus was viewed as a messenger "bearing the name of God." In this regard, anyone bearing the name of the Lord "represents the Father, he is one with the Father, through the agency of the name. Therefore he also bears the glory of God in the face as his angel."[20]

When the worshipper through Psalm 8 refers to the majesty of the name of the Lord over all the earth, he points to the protective presence of

---

[17] Raymond Jacques Tournay, *Seeing and Hearing God with the Psalms: The Prophetic Liturgy of the Second Temple in Jerusalem*, transl. J. Edward Crowley (Sheffield: Sheffield Academic Press, 1991), 108.
[18] Ibid.
[19] Crispin H.T. Fletcher-Louis, "The Gospel Thief Saying (Luke 12:39–40 and Matthew 24:43–44) Reconsidered," in Christopher Rowland and Crispin H.T. Fletcher-Louis (eds), *Understanding, Studying and Reading: New Testament Essays in Honour of John Ashton* (Sheffield Academic Press, 1998), 48–68, here 66.
[20] Jonathan Draper, "Practicing the Presence of God in John," in Jonathan Draper (ed.), *Orality, Literacy, and Colonialism in Antiquity* (Atlanta: Society Biblical Literature, 2004), 165.

God in the whole world. Such protective presence is more dependable than any other as the psalmist will say in another place: "Some take pride in chariots, and some in horses, but our pride is in the name of the Lord our God" (Ps 20:7). The psalmist presents the name of Yahweh, and not any created things including human beings, as the source of security for the whole earth. This becomes the frame within which human beings should think of themselves and others in the world.

THE MAJESTY OF YAHWEH (VV. 1B–2)

The worshipper in Psalm 8 goes on to exemplify the greatness of Yahweh in creation. Informed by the exaltation of the name of the Lord on all the earth in the prelude and postlude, we are introduced to the glory or splendor of the Lord that endows the heavens (v. 1b) and to the phrase: "Out of the mouths of babes and infants you have founded a bulwark because of your foes, to silence the enemy and the avenger" (Ps 8:2). It is not clear how one finds this "strength from a naturally weak and insignificant phenomenon, namely the utterances of a baby's mouth."[21] It is also not clear what group of children the psalm has in mind. Finally, one cannot decide easily how to translate עֹז or עֹז (oz): "strength," "stronghold," or "fortress/ bulwark"? Literary analysis is helpful here since the poetic technique of "utilizing an oxymoron" is employed in a way that "inculcates the notion of God's supreme power and creative ability to generate something potent and powerful out of nothing."[22] In this sense God's ability to create the powerful universe from nothing is represented with the "incompatibility of the strength-weakness union, and thus intensifies the power of the poetic imagery."[23]

From the perspective of our anthropological theme, we can see then that the frailest and most vulnerable state of being human is infancy as depicted in Psalm 8:2. Yet, because the protection and security of the human being, their fortress, from all forms of enemies comes from the mighty of Yahweh, human beings can consider themselves secure and safe even in their weakest moments. The "reference to enemies and the foe and the avenger in Psalm 8:3 hint at the fact that we live in messy world" but must trust Yahweh's "overriding, continuing care for humanity."[24]

---

[21] Emanuel, op cit. (note 8), 48.

[22] Ibid.

[23] Ibid.

[24] Carl J. Bosma, "Beyond 'Singers and Syntax': Theological and Canonical Reflections on Psalm 8," in W. Th. Van Peursen and J. W. Dyk (eds), *Tradition and Innovation in Biblical Interpretation* (Leiden: Brill, 2011), 90.

THE FRAGILITY OF THE HUMAN BEING (VV. 3–4)

This section underlines the greatness of the Lord by contrasting the size of creation with the insignificance of human beings. The power of Yahweh demonstrated in creation and the location in this creation of the human being helps the human being to have the right perspective of the self. Verses 3 and 4 are actually asking what the value of the human being is in the face of the enormity of the created universe. Verse 4 becomes the pivot and transitional rhetorical question: "what are human beings that you are mindful of them, mortals that you care for them?" What the psalmist does here is not to "deify creation" but provides a contrast "with the Egyptian view of the cosmos" that would take the "heaven, earth and the sky and the sun" as represented by the "deities Nut, Shu, Geb, and Ra, respectively."[25] It looks as if the worshipper of Psalm 8 would wish all human beings would, when they think too much of themselves, repeat verse 4: "what are human beings that you are mindful of them, mortals that you care for them?"

THE GREATNESS OF THE HUMAN BEING (VV. 5–8)

While verse 4 would be appropriate to put a self-exalting humanity in its place, verses 5–8 seek to exalt human beings in their humble state. Here human beings are presented as envoys of God—crowned with "glory and honor"—created in the image of God if one would use the language of Genesis 1. The general spirit of the response to the rhetorical question is that "it is the glory of God to form a frail man from the dust of the ground and then entrust dominion over the earth to him."[26] The greatness of human being derives from the greatness of God and in the God-given responsibility over all other creatures. The human being is here presented as having been made "a little lower than God" (v. 5), expressing the high position of humanity where "very little is kept" from them.[27]

That the human being is given dominion over "all three tiers of the cosmos, from the beasts of the field (i.e., earth), the birds of the heavens and the creatures of the seas"[28] is reminiscent of the creation story in Genesis 1, where the human being is presented as having responsibility for all created things.

---

[25] Hassel Bullock, op. cit. (note 10).

[26] Allen P. Ross, *A Commentary on the Psalms* (Grand Rapids: Kregel, 2011), 293.

[27] G. C. Berkouwer, *Studies in Dogmatics: Holy Scripture*, transl. Jack B. Rogers (Grand Rapids: Wm. B. Eerdmans, 1975), 224.

[28] Kyle Greenwood, *Scripture and Cosmology: Reading the Bible between the Ancient World and Modern Science* (Downers Grove: Inter Varsity Press, 2015), 114.

The human being is never God; they are made a little lower than God. Walter Brueggemann has helpfully pointed to the need to keep the authority given to human beings and human submission to the owner of creation together:

> The two must be held together. Praise of God without human authority is abdication and "leaving it all to God," which the psalm does not urge. But to use human power without the context of praise of God is to profane human regency over creation and so usurp more than has been granted. Human persons are to rule, but they are not to receive the ultimate loyalty of creation. Such loyalty must be directed only to God.[29]

POSTLUDE

The postlude reiterates the prelude with another praise of Yahweh. As has been observed above, the

> first and the last thought is about the glory of God. In this way the psalm demonstrates that everything points to God and that without doxology there can be no human dignity. Only when human beings are aware of their own insignificance can they recognize the greatness of God and will they be able to represent the Lord in the right way on earth.[30]

LUTHER AND THE HUMAN BEING

On 14 January 1536, Martin Luther took up a disputation guided by his forty theses where he addresses the notion of being human. The following theses give an insight into Luther's view of the person:

> 20. Theology to be sure from the fullness of its wisdom defines man as whole and perfect:

> 21. Namely, that man is a creature of God consisting of body and a living soul, made in the beginning after the image of God, without sin, so that he should procreate and rule over the created things, and never die,

> 22. But after the fall of Adam, certainly, he was subject to the power of the devil, sin and death, a twofold evil for his powers, unconquerable and eternal.

---

[29] Walter Brueggemann, *The Message of the Psalms* (Minneapolis: Augsburg, 1984), 38.
[30] James D. G. Dunn and John W. Rogerson (eds), *Eerdmans Commentary on the Bible* (Cambridge: Wm. B. Eerdmans, 2003), 373.

23. He can be freed and given eternal life only through the Son of God, Jesus Christ (if he believes in him).[31]

In this disputation Luther rejects other constructions of the human being that were proposed by different philosophies of his day. While Luther does not reject that the human being is a rational being, he chooses to address the human being as one who is justified by faith. In Bayer's words,

> To be human means to have undeserved existence, that which is purely indebted to another [...] .The existence of the human being is his elementary designation: one for whom life itself and whatever is necessary for life are given to him [...]—yet he cannot, even for a single blink of the eye, ever exist because of something that comes forth from within himself.[32]

This understanding of the human being as a graced being was Luther's special contribution to anthropology beyond theology. The general understanding of grace tends to be more theological and less social, political, economic and other such categories. For Luther, the human being lives from borrowed tools. This grace oriented anthropology should not inform how humans understand themselves as living before God, but also as living before other humans and creation. As Luther says in his "Small Catechism," "I believe that God has created me together with all that exists [...] And all this is done out of pure, fatherly, and divine goodness and mercy without any merit or worthiness of mine at all."[33] Luther recognized that being created was to partake with other creatures in the common life. Such a perspective prevents human beings from overestimating themselves. Even there where human beings have worked very hard and acquired things, they remember that it is God who has

> given me and still preserves my body and soul: eyes, ears, and all limbs and senses; reason and mental faculties. In addition, God daily and abundantly provides shoes and clothing, food and drink, house and farm, spouse and children, fields, livestock, and all property —along with all the necessities and nourishment for this body and life. God protects me against all danger and shields and preserves me from all evil.[34]

---

[31] *LW* 34, 138.

[32] Oswald Bayer, *Martin Luther's Theology: A Contemporary Interpretation*, transl. Thomas H. Trapp (Grand Rapids, MI: Wm. B. Eerdmans, 2008), 156.

[33] Robert Kolb and Timothy Wengert (eds), *The Book of Concord. The Confessions of the Evangelical Lutheran Church* (Minneapolis: Fortress Press, 2000), 354-55.

[34] Ibid.

The above depiction of the human being both in Psalm 8 and Luther raises questions about what this means for human agency. It has long been affirmed in social sciences that to be "a human being is to be an agent—although not all agents are human beings... ."[35] Here being an agent is understood as having "power" or the "transformative capacity, the capability to intervene in a given set of events so as in some way to alter them."[36] Both in the Psalm and Luther's perspective, human agency is better understood in relationship with God. For the psalms, any agency out of synch with what God is doing is futile: "Unless the Lord builds the house, those who build it labor in vain. Unless the Lord guards the city, the guard keeps watch in vain. It is in vain that you rise up early and go late to rest, eating the bread of anxious toil; for he gives sleep to his beloved" (Ps 127:1-2).

Such an understanding of human agency does not diminish human creativity and ingenuity but rather enhances them.

---

[35] Anthony Giddens, *The Nation-state and Violence* (Cambridge: Polity Press, 1985), 7.
[36] Ibid.

THE THREE SISTERS' GARDEN:
LIVING TOGETHER FOR THE COMMON GOOD

Mary Philip (Joy)

> Our dreams have been doctored. We belong nowhere. We sail unanchored on troubled seas. We may never be allowed ashore. Our sorrows will never be sad enough. Our joys never happy enough. Our dreams never big enough. Our lives never important enough. To matter. . ."[1]

This quote by Arundhati Roy, a compatriot of mine from India, echoes the sentiment of the days when crime, corruption, death and destruction were words that were all too familiar and hope seemingly distant. Then I read this quote, also by Arundhati Roy,

> The time has come, the Walrus said. Perhaps things will become worse and then better. Perhaps there's a small god up in heaven readying herself for us. Another world is not only possible, she's on her way. Maybe many of us won't be here to greet her, but on a quiet day, if I listen very carefully, I can hear her breathing.[2]

Maybe hope is not so distant after all. Arundhati's words evoke a *déjà vu*. Would Luther have felt this way in the sixteenth century? Is it time for another reformation? Five hundred years! Maybe it is time for another reformation. Things are definitely worse and so the bettering might be on the way. Well, all we have to do is work with this "small god up in heaven readying herself for us." However, it is easier said than done!

---

[1] Arundhati Roy, *The God of Small Things* (Toronto, Canada: Vintage, 1997), 52.
[2] Arundhati Roy, from the Lannan Foundation lecture "Come September," on 18 September 2002, at the Lannan Foundation in Santa Fe, New Mexico.

LUTHER AND THE ORDERS OF CREATION

What is the kind of relationship between theology, politics and economics that would advance the common good, and make another world possible? We just have to pick up the newspaper or watch the TV, or simply look around to know that the existing *modus operandi* is not working. So, how can this relationship be reconfigured? Lutherans are familiar with Luther's institutions or orders of creation—*ecclesia*, *politia* and *oeconomia*. With the creation of the birds and the animals and then with Adam and Eve, the household (*oeconomia*) was put in place, although not its governing rules. The entrusting of the well-being of the creatures with Adam and Eve saw the institution of civil society or the *politia* (though I know that Luther was ambiguous about this because there are places where he refers to the postlapsarian institution of *politia*). The Sabbath, the day God rested, is seen as the prefiguration of the church or the *ecclesia*. In Luther's words, "Three institutions (*Stände*) were ordained by God in which we live with God and good conscience. The first is the household; the other the political and worldly regime; the third the church or priestly order—all according to the three Persons of the Trinity."[3] These three orders were not independent of one another but safeguarded and supported each other by mutual participation. They worked together as "functions of the human society."[4] Malfunction, non-function or dysfunction of any one of the orders disturbed the balance of society for each had a vital role to play. The church was the vestibule for the proclamation of the Word of God, be it as gospel or law and/or both and for worship or for "human response to be expressed." The household or the *oeconomia* provided the sustenance. The household was the place where human relationships and human reproduction happened. This is also where human beings labored—produced goods and exchanged goods, where commerce happened—what we call modern economics. The *politia* or civil government was for the sake of social order, defense and protection. For Luther, politics and economics, to keep the terminology, and the church (theology as well) are ways in which human beings "cooperate with God." To use Phil Hefner's words, these are spaces and/or spheres where human beings are called to be created cocreators. Cocreation is not always life giving. And this is where theology plays a key role; theology has the dirty yet vital role of probing, questioning and challenging.

Luther uses two metaphors—instruments and masks—to explicate how this cooperation happens. An instrument is a tool that aids in our labors,

---

[3] Vítor Westhelle, *Transfiguring Luther: The Planetary Promise of Luther's Theology* (Eugene, OR: Cascade, 2016), 284.
[4] Ibid.

in our efforts to produce. Paul's usage of one body and many parts is a useful example here. The part, be it the hand or the head, becomes the representative of the whole. Speech is distinctive of humans. It actually happens because of the working together of respiratory, circulatory and nervous systems, yet it comes out of one part of the body, the mouth and is representative of the whole person. While the tool is applicable to the order of the household or the *oeconomia* or economics, the mask takes effect in *politia*.[5] The mask can be used to represent "the one who speaks on behalf of a cause, a person or a group representing and communicating interests on account of the common good."[6]

In Kerala, where I come from, there is an art form called Kathakali that in the past was a way of enacting stories from the Hindu scriptures to reinforce religious norms and values in the people. Today it has evolved to a level where the dancer or performer, depicting mainly political characters, through the role they portray calls attention to an existing societal problem. And the beauty is that the masks are not really masks.

The faces of the dancers are painted so intricately and dramatically that the human dancer-actors are transformed into characters they play. The heavy facial coloring almost makes the performers look as if they were wearing masks. Traditionally the *Kathakali* dancers/actors do not speak. The precise mudras or gestures and facial expressions of the dancers translate each word sung by singers in Sanskrit or in Manipravalam (a combination of Sanskrit and Malayalam).[7]

As mentioned earlier, both *oeconomia* and *politia* are orders of creation instituted by God. However, for Luther, they are not autonomous or neutral. They work together as is exemplified by the Kathakali. So, how does that happen? What is it that enables the part to represent the whole? Similarly, who or what is behind the mask? "If it is politics that administers the power relations, it is labor and *oeconomia* that sustains it."[8] Theology (or church) grounds both. While God does not require our works, we ourselves and our neighbors need it. There is value to our work—political, economic or religious—not as gaining access to salvation but as service to God and neighbor. Each one of us has a calling, a vocation, and vocation is more than what we do for money. It includes all the duties and responsibilities that are ours in all spheres of life that work towards the common good

---

[5] Ibid., 287.

[6] Ibid.

[7] The section on *Kathakali* is from my memory and also includes excerpts from various websites.

[8] Westhelle, op. cit. (note 3), 300.

and the caring of the world.[9] So, now we have the *modus operandi* for the interaction between politics, economics and theology in place—they need to work together. In other words, PET—the acronym for politics, economics and theology—cannot but work together! Going back to the question of how we can reconfigure the relationship between the three so that it can work, there is indeed an ingenious reconfiguration or replanting, so to speak.

I work best with metaphors or, in this case, should I say fables or parables. It gives me added vocabulary since the language I speak is not native to me. But I also know that there is a limit to what they can offer. So, beware, what I employ, be it metaphors, fables or parables, they are my way of presenting another perspective and it can take you only so far. And, most importantly, it is a perspective not the perspective. And it may not work for you. So, how do we replant the relationship between PET so that they work for the common good?

THE THREE SISTERS' GARDEN

The term "Three Sisters" emerged from the Iroquois creation myth. It was said that the earth began when "Sky Woman" who lived in the upper world became curious and looked through a hole in the sky and fell through it. The sea animals saw her coming, and the turtle rose up to hold her and thus broke her fall. They decided that she needed a place to stand on and so they decided to get earth from the only place that they knew had earth, which was at the bottom of the sea. One by one they dove under but none could get down to the abyss except for the otter. She took the plunge only to perish, or so the other animals thought. After four days she or rather her body came up. The sea animals pulled the unconscious otter up onto the turtle's back and when they pried her paws open they saw that she had some earth in it which became the "Turtle Island" and is now what is called North America. Sky woman had become pregnant before she fell. She gave birth to a daughter on the turtle island who grew up into a young woman, who also became pregnant (by the West wind). She died while giving birth to twin boys. Sky Woman buried her daughter in the "new earth." From her grave grew three sacred plants—corn, beans and squash. Corn, Beans and Squash are called the three sisters according to the First Nations people of Canada.[10]

---

[9] William Schumacher, "Faithful Witness in Work and Rest," in *Concordia Journal*, 41, 2, 136-50.

[10] The story is well known among the First Nations people in Canada and the text above is from my colleague, Dorinda Kruger Allen who is an Algonquin. According

"The Three Sisters," a Mohawk legend[11] is well known and it is believed that every indigenous child today knows these sisters. The little sister in green is the bean, her sister in yellow is the squash, and the eldest sister with long flowing hair of yellow and the green shawl is the corn.

The three sisters' garden is a way of planting that originated with the Haudenosaunee tribe. As the Iroquois legend goes corn, bean and squash, "the three Native maidens, are three inseparable sisters who grow only together. The three, while very different, love each other very much and thrive when they are near each other."[12]

The corn, tall and straight, supports the beans by providing a natural pole for bean vines to climb up. Bean vines thus form a framework around the corn, preventing it from falling over. The beans also help stabilize the corn plants, making them less vulnerable to being blown over in the wind. The big squash leaves cover the ground, conserving moisture and shading out weeds. Shallow-rooted squash vines become a living mulch, shading emerging weeds and preventing soil moisture from evaporating, and thereby improving the overall chances of the crops to survive in dry years. The spiny squash plants also help to keep predators away from the corn and beans. And just to put the icing on the cake, the beans, being legumes, have nitrogen fixing bacteria in their nodules and thus fix nitrogen in their roots and provide extra nitrogen for the corn and squash. This not only increases the overall fertility of the land but the crop residue from this planting combination is incorporated back into the soil at the end of the season, thereby building up the organic matter and improving the soil structure for the following years.[13]

The three sisters—corn, beans and squash—not only support each other but they also need each other. The combination of plants helps each one of them to produce fully. Furthermore, in terms of nutrition, they complement each other. Corn is low in protein but high in carbohydrates; the beans are rich in protein thus balancing the lack thereof it in corn. The squash is the source of both vitamins and fats in the form of oil from the seeds. The three plants are thus a nutrition powerhouse when combined. This is a classic example of three different entities living together for the

---

to her, these stories, myths, are not fixed. They are living and change according to the one who tell it.

[11] The story, titled "The Three Sisters," was recorded by Lois Thomas of Cornwall Island, Canada. It is one of a collection of legends compiled by students at Centennial College, Toronto, Canada.

[12] The text is taken from http://www.reneesgarden.com/articles/3sisters.html.

[13] Ibid.

common good. It is a lesson *par excellence* in creating a community where the members thrive while being independent as well as interdependent.[14]

The vegetables were not planted randomly. It is done in a specific way. Raised mounds are made in well hoed earth. Then the vegetables were planted in a systematic way. The corn is planted in the center of each mound, five or six corn kernels of corn is planted in a small circle. When the corn has grown to about five inches, beans are planted in a circle about six inches away from the corn kernels. When the beans sprout, which takes about a week, the pumpkin seeds are planted at the edge of the mound about a foot away from the beans. As the plants grow, some thinning of the seedlings is necessary and only the sturdiest of the corn, the bean and squash seedlings are kept. When the beans grow, it is made sure that they are supported by cornstalks by wrapping them around the corn. The squash will crawl out between the mounds, around the corn and beans.[15]

Thus the three sisters are either planted in raised mounds or in beds. The raised mounds are about 3–4 inches high, to improve drainage and soil warmth with a small crater at the top so the water does not drain off the plants quickly, thus helping to conserve water. Or else they are planted in beds with the soil raised around the edges, so that water collects in the beds. In other words, the design of the bed is adjusted according to the climate and type of soil. This cautionary note points to the importance of context.

Success with a three sisters' garden involves careful attention to timing, seed spacing, and varieties. In many areas, simply planting all three in the same hole at the same time, results in a snarl of vines and confusion and convolution will be the order!

CORNY POLITICS, BEANY ECONOMICS AND SQUASHY THEOLOGY

The connection between the three sisters' garden and the reconfiguration of the PET (politics, economics, theology) relationship should be obvious by now: the three sisters in this case are, politics, economics and theology. The corny politics, beany economics and squashy theology.

Politics becomes the pole or pillar for the exercising of power and distribution of resources; economics is the household or the network of relationships that is involved in the nurturing; and the task of theology is to be at the margins, the in-between or betwixt and between places as you saw in the three sisters' garden.

---

[14] Ibid.
[15] See http://www.nativetech.org/cornhusk/threesisters.html.

Politics is the backbone or the pillar that creates and administers laws that give freedom to human beings, be it the right of speech or clothing; of worship; for the protection of human rights; for promoting peace and justice for the poor, the oppressed and exploited. In addition, governance needs to be in place to facilitate commerce and create jobs so that the people can have the right to work and be productive and contributing members of the society that accords them the dignity and respect due to all human beings. Just as the corn stalk supports the bean that provides nourishment, our political system needs to be a pillar of support to those that make up our communities, those that nurture and sustain us. It is from the other two fields—economics and theology—that politics will derive its strength, vitality and authority and ultimately its legitimacy to make decisions for the common good.

Human beings are also economic units whose value is also measured in terms of production, including reproduction and consumption. Economics or *oeconomia* is about human activity performed in what humans think of as a web of relationships, or in other times of what we conceive of as home and work place. It is this web of relationships that provides the framework for *politia* so that it does not crumble and fall. Just as the beans provide nutrients for the corn and by virtue of the nitrogen fixing bacteria in their nodes fixes nitrogen for the soil, the household/*oeconomia* facilitates and promotes the growth by nurturing, sustaining, and exercising responsible stewardship over its resources. It is about creating a web of relationships where we care for the neighbor and the earth that hosts us with all its living and non-living members. This web of connectedness is made possible by the strong framework it provides for the political realm.

Squashy Theology: the role and place of theology

The place of theology is at the margins. Like the squash plants, the place of theology is lodged betwixt and between. To use Derrida's terminology they represent *choratic* spaces or else third spaces as Homi Bhabha would call them. To use the words of Bhabha, "these in-between spaces provide the terrain for elaborating strategies for selfhood—singular or communal that initiate new signs of identity ... in the act of defining the idea of [a new] society itself."[16] This is the role of theology *par excellence*. Being in these spaces "gives rise to something different, something new ..., a new area of negotiation of meaning and representation."[17] It is a place that facilitates

---

[16] Homi Bhabha, *Location of Culture* (New York: Routledge, 1994), 1–2.
[17] Jonathan Rutherford. "The Third Space, Interview with Homi Bhabha," in *Identity: Community, Culture, Difference* (London: Lawrence &Wishart, 1998), 211.

encounters and where meanings change,[18] where one is open to the other, be they our neighbor or politics or economics.[19] It is a place where newness enters, where one questions existing power structures. The third spaces are "a dialogical site," a place where enunciation, identification, and negotiation"[20] are possible. The Christian story takes place in the third space—the enunciation is to a lowly maiden's home (third space), the Creator identifies with the creature and the created order in the third space of the barn and place of the skull, Golgotha, also where the negotiation culminated.

Bhabha gives this poignant example of a third space: For his illustration, Bhabha employs the Gacaca courts that are community courts of justice set up in 2001 after the 1994 Rwandan genocide. For Bhabha, the Gacaca, the traditional grass mat in Rwanda from which the Gacaca courts derived their name, is a third space. According to him, the Gacaca is not just a neutral ground, where confession and confrontation of guilt takes place, but "a place and time that exists in-between the violent and the violated, the accused and the accuser, allegation and admission."[21] This mat where the two groups meet, this "site of in-betweenness", the third space, the gap, becomes the "ground of discussion, dispute, confession, apology and negotiation through which Tutsis and Hutus together confront the inequities and asymmetries of societal trauma not as a "common people" but as a people with a common cause."[22] Should not theology be in that space? Where else could it be?

These spaces are also spaces of limitless possibilities. The third space or the in-between spaces, are a

> limitless composition of lifeworlds that are radically open and openly radicalizable; ... that are never completely knowable but whose knowledge nevertheless guides our search for emancipatory change and freedom from domination. It is disorderly, unruly, constantly evolving ... the order.[23]

It is where life is lived in constant transformation, where there is daily dying and rising up—what we in the Christian world call baptism. The third space is the fissure where something "takes place," a space that allows for

---

[18] Ibid., 202.

[19] Bhabha, *Location of Culture*, op. cit. (note 16), 1–2.

[20] Bhabha, "In the Cave of Making: Thoughts on Third Space," in Karin Ikas and Gerhard Wagner (eds), *Communicating in the Third Space*, (New York: Routledge, 2009), x.

[21] Ibid.

[22] Ibid.

[23] Edward Soja, "Third Space," in *Communicating in the Third Space*, op. cit. (note 20), 54.

something to seep, to proliferate, to branch out, to augment, to bring forth something different. What takes place here unsettles our ways of thinking. It makes us realize that every impoverished person diminishes our own lives; it strikes our conscience that every refugee, every homeless person makes our homes a little less of a home; it makes us painfully aware that every human being who is trafficked chips away at the dignity that is ours. What happens there is an unhinging of order, organization, not to replace it with disorder or disorganization but to intervene, to insert a stutter, a pause within the expected, in other words, to create a cognitive dissonance, to provoke and thus evoke and finally convoke so that it allows for something different to happen. It does not even have to be new but something that was already there but not realized before.

In theology it is called revelation—to reveal/uncover something that was veiled. These spaces that theology is called to occupy are indeed epiphanic spaces; places of *parousia*, privileged places where God chooses to reveal Godself, where divine life is embodied in the very stuff of this world. They are spaces that God so loved that God surrendered God's space and became an inhabitant so that the spaceless may have a space and the voiceless a voice. And this is precisely where theology ought to be, constantly challenging, resisting and redefining, leading to a construction of a new meaning, a new order of justice, a new identity. Theology is called to be in such spaces where there is the possibility of being and becoming.

"All margins are dangerous. If they are pulled this way or that the shape of fundamental experience is altered. Any structure of ideas is vulnerable at its margins."[24] The margins, that is, theology, will determine if the center holds. In its unique position it calls the center into question. One of the tasks of theology is to have the mind of Thomas, to probe, to challenge and verify facts.[25] Theology thus is the conscience of the *politia* and *oeconomia*. Truth is put on trial at the border, in exactly the place of theology and it is this border that defines and redefines it. As the squash does, theology dares to stand at the boundary, transgressing it, and, at the same time, providing a cover, a safe haven for the truth to be told. Margins, or third spaces, or in between spaces are places where danger lurks, where predators prowl. But as Hölderlin says, where danger lurks that which saves also grows.[26] Remember how the spiny leaves of squash keep the predators away! But most importantly, the squashy theology seems to shade the soil from drying up under the scorching sun, the law, preserving the moisture, the gospel.

---

[24] Mary Douglas, *Purity and Danger* (New York: Routledge, 2002), 149–50.
[25] Systematic theology class at the Lutheran School of Theology at Chicago, 2001.
[26] Friedrich Hölderlin, *Hymns and Fragments* (New Jersey: Princeton University Press, 1984), 102.

The world that we live in, the earth, is the quintessence of the human condition. Politics, economics, and theology are the essential orders of the body of this world, *corpus mundi*. According to Hannah Arendt, there are three fundamental actions in our active life—labor, work and speech and they are fundamental because each corresponds to one of the basic conditions under which life on earth has been given to us.[27] And, we are creatures of labor. We see work as part and parcel of who and what we are and it comes out of love for what we do and intrinsic to our sense of worth and dignity as those created in the image of God. The work we do matters, because our work participates in the Creator's own work in the world.[28] It is also how we communicate with each other, to God and to the world around us. In other words, it is a sign of our connection to God and to one another. When we lose our connection to God, our connectedness to our creatureliness, to the earth, is also lost.

The three sisters' garden offers me a metaphoric fable for the interaction between theology, politics, and economics, especially for the role of theology. It is a space where the three live along side, not losing who or what they are but leaning on and leaking into each other, supporting and sustaining each other to create a public space where identity, purpose and meaning are created.[29] As human beings we need such spaces to serve as crucibles that reimagine, reconfigure and revitalize human lives so as creatively to engage in working toward the common good, to make another world possible. The theme for the 500th Anniversary of the Reformation is "Liberated by God's Grace." I think it would be worthwhile to ask ourselves some questions: Do our political, theological and economic discourses, the laws we administer, the relationships we forge do justice to our neighbors, the indigenous people of the land, to the neighboring nations? Do our ways of life, our production and consumption, rape the earth that nourishes and sustains us? Gandhi stated very truly that we need to learn to live more simply, so that others may simply live. There is enough on earth for everybody's need but not for everybody's greed.[30] As people liberated by God's grace, are our actions and words liberating for others? Do they lead to liberation or bondage? The role of theology is thus to reform, reshape,

[27] These do not correspond to the three orders of Luther.
[28] Schumacher, op cit. (note 9), 149.
[29] David Pfrimmer, "Stewards of the Public Commons: A Vocation for Government and Church," in Karen L. Bloomquist (ed.), *Communion, Responsibility, Accountability: Responding as a Lutheran Communion to Neoliberal Globalization*, LWF Documentation 50/2004 (Geneva: The Lutheran World Federation, 2004), 235.
[30] See Martin Kopp, "Responsible Stewards of God's Creation" in Anne Burghardt (ed.) *Creation—Not for Sale* (Leipzig: Evangelische Verlagsanstalt, 2015), 39.

reconfigure, replant our ways of thinking and living and worshipping so that we are enabled "to see faith and not crippled feet or lame bodies;"[31] so that we are empowered to do more than just stand but jump and walk.

While we live on this earth, we leak into each other like different flavors during cooking.[32] My story will leak into yours and others' into mine. It needs to. That is what happens when PET work together as in the three sisters' garden. Then, together with Arundhati Roy we can also say,

> The time has come, the Walrus said. Perhaps things will become worse and then better. Perhaps there's a small god up in heaven readying herself for us. Another world is not only possible, she's on her way. Maybe many of us won't be here to greet her ... .[33]

But, maybe, if PET work together as in the three sisters' garden, "on a quiet day, if we listen very carefully, we can hear her breathing."[34] Another world is necessary; together we can make it possible.[35]

---

[31] From Bishop Kameeta's sermon at the opening worship of the international conference "Global Perspectives on the Reformation: Interactions between Theology, Politics and Economics," 28 October 2015, Windhoek, Namibia.
[32] Salman Rushdie, *Midnight's Children* (Berkshire: Vintage, 1995), 38.
[33] Roy, op. cit. (note 2).
[34] Ibid.
[35] The theme for the 2016 World Social Forum in Montreal.

THE APPLE TREE UNDER THE RAINBOW

Jaana Hallamaa

> Whoever comes to me and does not hate father and mother, wife and children, brothers and sisters, yes, and even life itself, cannot be my disciple. Whoever does not carry the cross and follow me cannot be my disciple.
>
> For which of you, intending to build a tower, does not first sit down and estimate the cost, to see whether he has enough to complete it? Otherwise, when he has laid a foundation and is not able to finish, all who see it will begin to ridicule him, saying, "This fellow began to build and was not able to finish."
>
> Or what king, going out to wage war against another king, will not sit down first and consider whether he is able with ten thousand to oppose the one who comes against him with twenty thousand? If he cannot, then, while the other is still far away, he sends a delegation and asks for the terms of peace. So therefore, none of you can become my disciple if you do not give up all your possessions (Lk 14:26-33).

What is Christian accountability? In what way have we been called to participate in bearing responsibility for the difficulties that our world is currently facing? Luke 14:26-33 challenges those thinking about following Christ. Not only are the prerequisites for discipleship hard—one must be prepared to hate those whom one loves most—one should also pause in order carefully to consider the consequences of this step. The decision to follow Jesus should and cannot be made before serious consideration and a thorough assessment of the costs. Otherwise one may face the fate of those whose ventures fail and who fall prey to the ridicule of others.

There are a plethora of ways in which Christians have met the challenge of discipleship. The Roman Catholic Church emphasizes the role of faith communicated through the church and its teaching. Following Christ takes place through the sacraments. It is first and foremost the Pope and the bishops who interpret what the Word of God demands and how the people of today must act when they follow Christ.

The Protestant tradition has typically laid emphasis on individual responsibility. We cannot escape the challenge Jesus puts to us by hiding behind the ecclesial authorities. It is each and every one of us who must personally face the call of Christ. One has to follow Christ and carry one's cross, whatever the cost. The emphasis is often on sacrifice: look what God has given to you—his only Son. Likewise, you, too, must be prepared to give up everything for the sake of the discipleship of Christ.

In the following I shall discuss some issues related to economics, accountability and participation on the basis of Luke 14. I must confess that after several readings I find this text to be perplexing as well as difficult. What Jesus demands is so extreme that I am almost appalled by it.

The gospels often depict Jesus calling people to become his followers. The encounter with Jesus usually leads to a call made by him and an immediate answer from the addressee. There is no time to deliberate; one must immediately get up and follow Jesus. Peter, Jacob and John leave their nets; Matthew and Levi abandon their occupation, rise and live up to the call. In Luke 14, Jesus describes the process of following him in other terms. Discipleship should not be adopted lightly but only after serious consideration—just as we would do if we had to choose an overarching plan for our lives.

What are the economics, accountability and participation of Christian discipleship, and how are they connected to the problems we face in today's world? Since the present text deals with the economics of following Christ, I will begin with that. We cannot speak about economics without dealing with accountability: only people who deal wisely with economics deserve to be regarded as being accountable. Accountability is also closely linked to participation: we are accountable not only for the assets with which we have been entrusted but also for our actions and their consequences.

TRUE DISCIPLESHIP OR THE ECONOMICS OF SALVATION

Nordic Lutherans are often blamed for having watered down the true meaning of Christianity. We are accused of concentrating on earthly matters instead of proclaiming the message of eternal salvation. This is taken as a sign of unbelief and ignoring the heart of the gospel. Should one not rather concentrate on talking about mission and evangelization instead of economic injustice and global warming? Have we lost the point of the economics of salvation and turned it into the economics of material welfare?

I wish to take this criticism seriously and learn from Christians who concentrate on salvation as the center of their faith. The purpose of following Christ is to participate in the promises of the gospel of salvation. Being accountable therefore means that we have to follow Christ in order to be saved. Accountability also implies a concern for others: they also should be saved. From this perspective, participation is first and foremost seen as spending time with fellow believers and converting nonbelievers so that they, too, become believers. Living the life of the saved implies turning one's interest in earthly things into heavenly concerns. Our life here in this world is only a foretaste of the things to come and, in this sense, not "the real thing." As we live our lives, we should keep in mind that the best is yet to come.

From this perspective, global warming, economic difficulties and the refugee crisis are not our biggest worries. Perhaps their true significance does not lie in the need to resolve them. Many Christians take our global problems as an apocalyptic sign of the approaching "last days" instead of acknowledging them as acute problems to be dealt with. For such Christians, the economics of salvation involves preparing oneself for the final battle between Christ and the Devil.

According to websites such as "Rapture Insurance" and "You've been left behind," true discipleship involves, first and foremost, conversion. Then one should stockpile canned provisions and other foodstuffs. In addition, Christians are called to exchange their assets for silver coins and gold bars, investments that are likely to retain their value despite fluctuating financial markets. All this should be done in preparation for the time of persecution that Christians will face in the near future.

The emphasis on the "real Christian message" of salvation that the true believers will enjoy after their death and the destruction of this world leads to strange consequences: forsaking everything for the sake of Jesus implies an obligation to equip oneself with both silver and material belongings in preparation for the ordeals of the apocalypse. What happens to the rest of the people and the world is of little importance. Those who do not convert are left to Satan to be eternally tormented, a fate they deserve.

The emphasis on celestial salvation raises moral concerns. Concentrating on eternal life produces a very narrow view of neighborly love. The material concerns of billions of people, as well as injustice, poverty and the like receive no attention, as the focus is on the fate of one's own soul and, thereafter, possibly on the duty to convert others to join the ranks of the tiny flock of the eternally blessed. There is no place for compassion for the suffering and still less for the improvement of their lot. Thus concentrating on one's own salvation only ends up with extreme narrowness and selfishness. The promise of the gospel is diminished to worrying about one's own eternal destiny.

Even a short analysis of this type of economics of salvation reveals how shallow it is. It diminishes the joyous message of Christianity, which becomes a petty investment in personal self-interest. The view of account-ability is narrowed down to taking care of one's own salvation and preparing oneself for a time of material austerity.

IMITATIO CHRISTI AS THE ECONOMICS OF FAITH

The concern about the fate of one's soul does not seem to be an accountable way of leading a Christian life. We need to shift our perspective from our-selves to Christ. As Christ is our ultimate example of faith and faithfulness, can we meet the challenge of accountability by asking what Jesus would do? What would Jesus do was a US-based movement in the 1990s designed to help young Christians figure out how to live as a Christian and how to act in problematic situations.

Asking what Jesus would do is a modern version of *imitatio Christi*, following Christ by becoming like him through emulation. Here the eco-nomics of faith involves asking this question in order to overcome the dilemmas one encounters in one's personal life. One's ability to follow the principle, What would Jesus do? would count as accountability, and joining like-minded others could be seen as Christian participation culminating in discipleship and the carrying of one's cross.

What would Jesus do in terms of economic injustice? We can use the Bible to find ways of answering this, but there are other problems that prove to be more difficult to resolve. What about global warming, the use of the Internet, the spread of multinational corporations and the like? Should we ignore such topics or can we rely on our development to become Christ-like as a way of finding the correct answers? How can we communicate the answers formulated by the, What would Jesus do? method to others who do not share our religious commitments?

Following Christ and being true to the Word of God are cornerstones of evangelical Christianity. Not unlike the slogan, What would Jesus do? these, too, have often become parodic material for stand-up comedians rather than central features of Christian life. Following Christ connotes pious self-examination, not vigorous and effective public activity. Living in accordance with the Word of God is often connected with a special interest in sexual ethics, not with an insatiable urge for justice or a vigilant aware-ness of the harmful consequences of human activity in nature.

What would Jesus do? is not and should not be a parodic question for us Lutherans. Still, it is not quite the way in which to approach questions. The traditional Lutheran way of dealing with moral dilemmas and political issues follows the lines of the doctrine of the two kingdoms. The ethical ideals of the New Testament, especially those formulated in the Sermon on the Mount, go beyond the possibilities and realities of our sinful world. As Christians we should act with selfless love, but as bearers of different offices and tasks in society, we must—in most cases—obey the law and preserve order.

Our tradition has guided us to think that neighborly love is mainly reserved for alleviating individual needs in crisis situations. Decency, following traditional ways of life and thought—not radicalness and awareness of moral problems—have been characteristics associated with the Lutheran version of following Christ. Economics, accountability and participation traditionally sound like political and not religious terms to our ears.

Resources of discipleship

Is this really all we have to offer for the economy of discipleship, accountability of faith and participation in the suffering of the world? To be able to bear economic responsibility, we need resources, and it is first and foremost the use of resources that is the criterion of accountability. Let us have a closer look at the kinds of resources our tradition has to offer us.

The British moral philosopher Jonathan Glover has designed a concept of moral resources in his impressive book, *Humanity: A Moral History of the Twentieth Century*. By moral resources he means ways of thinking and acting that prevent us from evil actions, heinous ways of behavior and mindlessness. Moral resources offer a basis for thinking and acting in critical situations where the moral compasses we use in deliberation do not work well.

I would like to bring forth something from our traditional common treasury. In his "Large Catechism," Martin Luther tells us to read every day, over and over again, the three basic texts of faith, i.e., the Apostolic Creed, the Ten Commandments and the Our Father. We also have the sacraments and the liturgical services. The basic texts and the Christian rituals are the moral resources given to us by the Lutheran tradition for Christian economics, accountability and participation; I do not think we have to go any further to search for them. My hope is to rediscover in these resources the help we need to meet the challenge of Christian discipleship and the extremely difficult demands posed by the text of Luke 14.

The Ten Commandments are often presented as a list of basic moral principles. When Jesus was challenged with the question regarding the greatest commandment of the law (Mt 22:37–40), he did not simply quote the Decalogue but said that one should love God with all one's will, might and strength, and one's neighbor as oneself. Luther gives the same answer by stressing that the most important commandment is the first: I am the Lord your God, You shall have no other gods before me.

The Ten Commandments are often described as containing universal moral rules. How can this be reconciled with the first commandment being the core and heart of the Decalogue? According to Luther, we always have a god whom we serve and according to whom we direct our lives. The criterion for who our god is, is not our creed, the values and principles we confess orally, but what we do and how we live. We find the criteria for following the first commandment in Matthew 25:

> When the Son of Man comes in his glory, and all the angels with him, then he will sit on the throne of his glory. All the nations will be gathered before him, and he will separate people one from another as a shepherd separates the sheep from the goats, and he will put the sheep at his right hand and the goats at the left.
>
> Then the king will say to those at his right hand, "Come, you that are blessed by my Father, inherit the kingdom prepared for you from the foundation of the world; for I was hungry and you gave me food, I was thirsty and you gave me something to drink, I was a stranger and you welcomed me, I was naked and you gave me clothing, I was sick and you took care of me, I was in prison and you visited me."
>
> Then the righteous will answer him, "Lord, when was it that we saw you hungry and gave you food, or thirsty and gave you something to drink? And when was it that we saw you a stranger and welcomed you, or naked and gave you clothing? And when was it that we saw you sick or in prison and visited you?" And the king will answer them, "Truly I tell you, just as you did it to one of the least of these who are members of my family, you did it to me" (Mt 25:31–40).

It is quite striking that the criteria for fulfilling the first and most important commandment are not a list of signs of piety and a definition of orthodox faith but rather a description of simple deeds of neighborly love. In the story of Matthew, the blessed ones do not even know that they have fulfilled the will of God and that they are thereby welcome to the eternal kingdom. The challenge of calculating the costs of following Christ seem indeed hard to meet, as the normal criteria of determining the price do not seem to apply here.

Being saved by Christ is often made to sound like something very special and extraordinary. And it may, indeed, be so. Christians are in this world but not of this world. The awareness of being elect and thereby something special may make Christians liable to isolating themselves from others in a way that Jesus depicts in his parable of the two visitors to the temple, the Pharisee and the tax collector (Lk 18:9–14). At the center of the Pharisee's piety, as described in the story, was contentment in not being like the tax collector but something pleasing in the eyes of God. Stressing one's special position in God's plan may even make us violate the first commandment. It is not God but the difference between ourselves and others that we concentrate on and place at the center of our faith.

We are not like the chosen ones at the Last Judgment, depicted in Matthew 25, whose encounters with Christ were not known to them. Instead, we find ourselves in the position of Peter, who claimed to be different from all others: even if everyone else should forsake Christ, he would not, not even at the peril of death. It is very easy to commit the fallacy of St Peter, *etiam si omnes, ego non*, even if all others, not I (Mt 26:33).

Exempting oneself from the common human condition violates central cornerstones of the Christian faith. We should never sever ourselves from the rest of creation. The first thing that we confess in the creed is that God is the Father, the giver and the source of all and everything. Our special place is based on the divine gifts that God the Creator freely and lovingly bestows upon creatures, all those who are bound together thanks to being part of creation. By acknowledging God as the Creator of all things, we also acknowledge what God confirms in Genesis: All was good (Gen 1).

The fundamental goodness of creation makes it a gift, shared not only by us but by everyone else as well. The given perfection of God's works also obliges us to mind and cherish its goodness. It is with joy and gratefulness that we can receive the gifts of creation, even in the midst of imperfection and sin.

There is sin and we should not forget that. The "but" of sin very quickly enters the discussion if we are true to the heritage of the Reformation. Sin not only casts a shadow over our existence, but also constitutes an impenetrable wall of obstacles between the perfection of creation and our present condition. Because of sin, everything has become corrupt and degenerate.

How far should we go in our emphasizing of the effects of sin? Does underlining the sinful nature of our worldly life, in fact, contravene one of the pillars of faith? Sin that covers everything represents the perverse realm of God's adversary. By concentrating on speaking about the sinful nature of our reality, do we not actually celebrate the devil and his works instead of celebrating God's greatness?

The life of faith is often called pious, and piety is identified with abstinence and self-denial. They are taken as the signs of carrying one's cross and following Jesus. Denouncing what people naturally cherish and enjoy is seen as the price true Christians pay for their faithfulness to the divine call. This emphasis is made stronger by reminding us of how much injustice and inequality there is. How can we enjoy the air-conditioned luxuries of a good hotel when millions of our neighbors must live their entire lives without a proper shelter? How many tons of carbon dioxide are produced due to international meetings that bring together Lutherans from different parts of the world?

On the whole, such questions lead nowhere. They sound correct and pious but do not actually help to change anything. Still, they show how we are incapacitated by sin, which is the central anti-resource in our lives. One of its perverse effects is that we get "stuck" to it. "But we are sinners," is a counterargument that can stop any constructive suggestion. It is easy to be paralyzed by one's sinfulness. We may even find perverse enjoyment in lamenting about our corrupt nature and inability to achieve anything good. It is nearly as common an effect of sin as concentrating on the sins of our neighbors.

We know grace to be the antidote to sin. It is typical of many churches and denominations of the Reformation tradition to celebrate the effects of grace and the renewing power of the Holy Spirit: Christians represent the people of God and their ways are truly different from the sinful world. We Lutherans are nevertheless typically not as confident as many of our fellow Christians about this—the famous principle *simul iustus et peccator* serves to remind us of this. Rather than claiming to be different from the rest of humankind, we stress the similarity. We are all bound together by a double bind, by creation and, likewise, the Fall. Our way to grace does not so much go straight through the exalted experience of the Pentecost as through the promises of baptism and the ever-recurrent act of the confession of sins.

The confession of sins as part of our liturgy is often seen as a minor and insignificant detail, at least in my part of the Lutheran world. I think that we are very mistaken here. This liturgical element is actually a powerful tool in our collection of moral resources. The confession of sins parallels the First Commandment and the first paragraph of faith in the Confession of Faith. There is no exception to our involvement in common human sinfulness. It is I and we who lie in the shackles of sin, and there we are together with the rest of humankind.

The confession of sins basically means acknowledging the facts. There is no escape, no "but, but, but" as an excuse. The acknowledging of facts is confirmed by the confession of sins that exposes us in a twofold manner: we are guilty before our neighbors and before God.

The confession of sins is followed by a condemnatory sentence, not by belittlement of what has happened and without a list of mitigating circumstances. There is no one to say that it does not matter and it can be forgotten. No, it does matter, and cannot be forgotten. Rather, we must face it. For this reason, grace in the form of the forgiveness of sins is not a bandage to cover but not to heal a wound. Grace in the form of forgiveness is mercy for the guilty who are set free.

We are set free, constantly and over and over again. Set free not to hoard canned food, silver coins and gold bars for the Apocalypse, but to plant an apple tree. The saying "If I knew that tomorrow was the end of the world, I would plant an apple tree today!" does not originate from Luther but is a very Lutheran slogan. It binds creation and the Apocalypse together.

It confirms the goodness of God's works and the value of human labor. It opens a perspective through which this day and the last one come together: God's future suffuses the hour that is present to us now.

What does all of this have to do with economics, accountability and responsibility? How is it connected to the challenge of the discipleship of Jesus that I began with? The economics of the apple tree does not amount to the accountability of the self-sacrificing heroism of an ascetic or a self-denying missionary. The economics of the apple tree does not play down the troubles of poverty and inequality, or belittle their meaning. It does not provide a miraculous solution to the grave problems of climate change that we are facing more acutely day by day.

The economics of the apple tree makes us accountable as human beings created and redeemed by God. We share the gift of life, the realities of sin and the promise of a world to come with everyone else on the globe. We have the resources of faith to follow Christ, who has carried the cross for us. The cross is the apple tree of love above from which the promises of God shine like the rainbow of hope for Noah and his family (Gen 9:17).

Communion and Mutual Accountability

Stephanie Dietrich

Introduction

The background to my comments on communion and mutual accountability is my experience with multilateral dialogues, such as the World Council of Churches' (WCC) Faith and Order Commission and the global and regional bilateral dialogues in which the Lutheran World Federation (LWF) or my own church, the Church of Norway, participate. It has been my experience that it is far easier to reach a certain degree of agreement on doctrinal issues in a bilateral dialogue. Representing a Lutheran church, such as the Church of Norway, or the LWF, as a confessional family in which all the member churches are in pulpit and altar fellowship (i.e., communion according to a Lutheran understanding), is a good and solid starting point in many ecumenical encounters. For many traditional mainstream churches, such as the Orthodox and Roman Catholic churches, which tend to encounter the Reformation churches with some degree of suspicion, the Lutheran tradition often seems to be perceived as being an "acceptable" dialogue partner.

Participating in Lutheran gatherings within the framework of the LWF feels a bit like coming home, like returning to my family. This could possibly constitute an additional approach to the theme "communion and mutual accountability": life within the Lutheran communion as LWF family life.

Limits and possibilities of the family metaphor

Most of us have not chosen our family; they are given to us and we to them. Most of us have not chosen our church affiliation either. The majority of church members are born into families belonging to a certain church tradition and within a specific church context. Converting to another church tradition may be perceived almost like "changing one's mother," which one usually does not do, even if there are serious challenges in one's relationship to her. In contexts such as the Nordic one or in traditionally "Lutheran countries," citizenship and church membership have to a large extent overlapped since the Reformation. This has radically changed in the last decades, also in the Nordic context.

Despite the obvious limits of applying the "family" metaphor to the life within a church communion, and in the full awareness that families are far from being ideal entities or places, I shall discuss in this paper some aspects of the family metaphor as a useful contribution to what it means to be a member of the LWF. Despite sometimes being a place of abuse and instability, families often are and should be places that offer a sense of belonging and strong bonds of mutual support and mutual accountability.

I find one aspect of the family metaphor useful, also in the context of the global Lutheran family: families are bound together by their common history. Families are still families, even when they are in deep trouble. Family members are obliged to care for one another. And, finally, coming back to the image of a mother: one's mother is given to one; normally one does not replace her. In this way, one might also say that the Lutheran church is "my mother," and therefore I am a part of the communion of churches within the LWF. This also implies that I have to struggle for its life and do whatever is in my power to make it a good place for living and supporting one another.

For many people, the family is a place where one always has a basic connection and relation to people who care for one and who one cares for, notwithstanding whether one personally likes them, or not. In my opinion, the most important aspect of living in a family is the fact that one is obliged to relate to one another in an accountable and reliable way. In both a human family and a church family, being a member includes shared responsibility and mutual accountability.

What does it mean that the LWF is not merely a fellowship or federation of churches, but a communion of churches? It is important to remind ourselves of the profound change in the self-understanding of the LWF, when the LWF Assembly at Curitiba in 1990 decided on this explicit change in its self-understanding.[1] Moving from federation to communion

---

[1] See "Constitution of The Lutheran World Federation," in Norman A. Hjelm (ed.) *I Have Heard the Cry of My People, Curitiba 1990. Proceedings of the Eighth Assembly*, LWF Report 28/29 (Geneva: The Lutheran World Federation, 1990), 141.

has had important implications, both for us as for our churches and for our encounter with the ecumenical world.

Thus, it is well worth reflecting on what it means to be a communion of churches, and how that influences our ecclesiological self-understanding and life together. As Martin Junge underlines,

> Since its beginnings, the LWF has grown tangibly in ecclesial density. This is visible in its structures and practices: it can be seen in the constitutional texts and governing structures, as well as in how it meets, works and celebrates together.[2]

Thus, the concept of "ecclesial density" needs to be developed in order to get an even clearer understanding of what it means to be a communion of churches.

The Lutheran communion—gift and task

The study document *The Self-Understanding of the Lutheran Communion—A Study Document* gives an outline of the Lutheran communion as both gift and task. The gift lies in the oneness in Christ, grounded in the apostolic tradition, finding its expression through mutual learning and sharing of the sacraments. This unity is understood as unity in reconciled diversity. Both the term "unity" and "reconciled diversity" need to be precisely defined. What do we mean by reconciled? Where are the boundaries of diversity? What do we mean by unity? Unity is more than a mere doctrinal agreement, and does not necessarily imply structural union. Nevertheless, unity demands visibility in a shared life and mutual accountability.

Our communion is a task because it challenges us to live this communion in all aspects of life—both in the church and in the world. Communion is not just an idea. It needs "to become historically manifest, visible and recognizable to the world."[3] This also includes the service to the world, diakonia, "which is an integral part of our identity and unifies us in the life of the communion."[4] In my opinion, the Lutheran communion has the task constantly to spell out what we mean by understanding diakonia as an important aspect and integral part of our identity. This is particularly relevant in light of the fact that the Reformation heritage with its emphasis

---

[2] Martin Junge, "Preface," in *The Self-Understanding of the Lutheran Communion. A Study Document* (Geneva: The Lutheran World Federation, 2015), 5.
[3] Ibid., 12
[4] Ibid.

on justification by faith alone has sometimes led to a narrowing down of our theological self-understanding.

The ecumenical achievements of the bilateral dialogues and agreements reached with the Roman Catholic Church on these issues clearly show that there is a basic agreement between our traditions on the need to hold together justification and sanctification. This can be helpful in terms of developing a fresh self-understanding within the Lutheran communion. Furthermore, the achievements of the Lutheran–Orthodox dialogue, underlining the links between the concepts of justification, sanctification and deification, need to be taken into account. The LWF's publication, *Diakonia in Context*,[5] emphasized that the church's identity is essentially a diaconal one. According to the Lutheran understanding, diakonia is one of the marks of the church.

> Diakonia is thus an intrinsic element of being Church and cannot be reduced to an
> activity by certain committed persons or made necessary by external social conditions.
> Diakonia is deeply related to what the Church celebrates in its liturgy and announces
> in its preaching. In the same way, liturgy and proclamation relate to diakonia.[6]

THE LEUENBERG MODEL: PULPIT AND ALTAR FELLOWSHIP

Describing the core aspects of being in communion in terms of pulpit and altar fellowship is not new. It is well known from the 1973 Leuenberg Agreement that distinguishes between church fellowship, based on consensus in the understanding of the gospel, and the realization of this fellowship in common witness and service. The Leuenberg fellowship—today called Community of Protestant Churches in Europe (CPCE)—has over many years tried to explore its self-understanding as a community that includes pulpit and altar fellowship and its belonging to a fellowship of churches shaped by the Reformation era. The CPCE, including over 100 mainly European member churches, is based on this common agreement. Without examining in detail the theological basis for this agreement, it is nonetheless interesting to follow the CPCE's discussions concerning its self-understanding as a community of churches. The common doctrinal agreement is the basis for pulpit and altar fellowship; it opens up for communion and cooperation. Nevertheless, this communion has to come to life and become visible in the world in order to become relevant for the life of the churches. It must be embodied in mutual

---

[5] Kjell Nordstokke (ed.), *Diakonia in Context: Transformation, Reconciliation, Empowerment. An LWF Contribution to the Understanding and Practice of Diakonia* (Geneva: The Lutheran World Federation, 2009).
[6] Ibid., 29.

accountability, common commitment, study processes, lived life and church practice—otherwise it is just a piece of paper. Communion needs to be a visible and living communion, in one or the other sense. In recent years, the CPCE has emphasized the understanding of communion as a worshipping community and the call to witness and service in the world. The declaration of being in communion has to go hand in hand with its being lived out in our societies. This applies both to the CPCE and the LWF.

As long as there is no real commitment to live and work together, the impact of a common agreement on doctrinal issues is rather limited. Within the framework of the CPCE, a number of churches, especially minority churches, called and still call for a stronger governing body, or even a decision-making body, such as a synod. Having represented the Church of Norway on the CPCE's presidium from 2006–2012, I would like to highlight some of the reasons why the idea of a European Protestant synod did not seem to make sense. One of the reasons for this skepticism is the conviction that being in communion as churches is primarily a moral not a legal obligation. Binding structures might certainly sometimes be helpful but, in the end, communion becomes lived communion only through the commitment of its members. What counts is the will to invest in its life. What needs to be examined is in which way this "being in communion" can actually become more important for the churches, so that it becomes relevant for our identity and existence in our respective societies as well as globally. This question is also relevant in the context of the LWF. Are we as member churches willing to invest in its life and thereby to make it a living communion in witness and service? How do we stand together in difficult times and support each other, even if there is disagreement on specific issues among us?

THE LUTHERAN HERITAGE—GIFT AND CHALLENGE

One of the aspects that needs further exploration is how, as churches within the LWF, we can connect more closely to the core doctrine of the Reformation—the doctrine of justification—and our understanding of the church's life in the world and our walking together.

This challenge is evident in study documents such as *The Church: Towards a Common Vision*, compiled by the Faith and Order Commission of the World Council of Churches,[7] and currently discussed in many of our

---

[7] *The Church: Towards a Common Vision*, Faith and Order Paper no. 214 (Geneva: WCC Publications, 2013), at https://www.oikoumene.org/en/resources/documents/commissions/faith-and-order/i-unity-the-church-and-its-mission/the-church-towards-a-common-vision

churches. It is obviously difficult to come to terms with the question of how doctrinal agreements actually relate to the way our churches live together in the different contexts of the world. Thus, the document is somehow divided into two separate parts: chapters 1–3 deal with doctrinal questions, and chapter 4 with the church's life in the world. The traditional discussion on the relationship between "faith and order" and "life and work" is still not resolved—neither in the WCC nor the Lutheran communion, the LWF. However, Lutherans need to be concerned about this disparity, precisely because of the in-depth discussions that have taken place on some of our core doctrines such as the doctrine of justification and the doctrine of two realms. I am convinced of the necessity of these doctrines for the reform and reformation of the medieval church. I am also concerned about the need to emphasize the contextuality of the Reformation doctrine and to develop it in light of a broader biblical perspective and 2000 years of church history in order to avoid a reductionist and fundamentalist reading of the Lutheran confessional writings.

Reading several LWF documents thoroughly, one realizes that there is a profound emphasis on the church's responsibility for witness and service to the world. Nevertheless, it seems that the important emphasis on the core message of the Reformation sometimes hinders a broader reading and understanding of our own ecclesiology. The emphasis on justification as the article by which the church stands or falls (*justificatio est articulus stantis et cadentis ecclesiae*)[8] defines our identity, even though the dialogue between the Roman Catholic Church and the LWF, and other ecumenical dialogues, have brought us much further in developing a broader understanding of the doctrine. Still, the basic dichotomy between justification and sanctification, as crucial as it was during the Reformation and has been ever since, also challenges us when we try to develop a more holistic ecclesiology, where the faith and life of the church are fully integrated.

Increasing ecclesial density, in my opinion, is very much about the capacity to hold together the declaration and realization of communion, the doctrine of justification and the doctrine of sanctification, the church's faith and the church's life.

Communion grows deeper in its "ecclesial density" when churches stand together in witness and service, also in challenging situations.

---

[8] *WA* 40/3.352.3, *"quia isto articulo stante stat Ecclesia, ruente ruit Ecclesia"* (Because if this article [of justification] stands, the church stands; if this article collapses, the church collapses).

CONCLUSION

I still remember a remarkable moment during one of the meetings of the Lutheran–Orthodox Joint Commission, when members of the Orthodox delegation, questioning the ecclesiality of the churches within the LWF, realized that the LWF understands itself as a communion, not a fellowship or federation, and that this implies pulpit and altar fellowship. Pulpit and altar fellowship refers to the basic notions of the church's identity as described in the *Confessio Augustana,* Article VII: Concerning the Church.[9] For the Orthodox, it made a difference that their dialogue partners were not just representatives of single churches belonging to the Lutheran tradition, but churches that are in full communion with each other, recognize each other's ministries and participate in the celebration of the sacraments and proclamation. Even if we are not one church, we are more than just churches living alongside each other. There is some kind of "churchiness," or "ecclesial density," attached to our being a communion.

Maybe we have to spell out even more precisely how the gift of being in communion becomes even more visible in our common life in the world through our common holistic mission. Understanding *diakonia* as a mark of the church might be helpful in this search for a deepened experience of being a communion and living it out.

---

[9] "The church is the assembly of saints in which the gospel is taught purely and the sacraments are administered rightly. And it is enough for the true unity of the church to agree concerning the teaching of the gospel and the administration of the sacraments." "The Augsburg Confession, Article VII: Concerning the Church," Latin text, in Robert Kolb and Timothy J. Wengert (eds), *The Book of Concord. The Confessions of the Evangelical Lutheran Church* (Minneapolis: Fortress Press, 2000), 43.

APPENDIX: MESSAGE FROM THE LUTHERAN WORLD FEDERATION INTERNATIONAL CONFERENCE

"GLOBAL PERSPECTIVES ON THE REFORMATION: INTERACTIONS BETWEEN THEOLOGY, POLITICS AND ECONOMICS"

28 OCTOBER–1 NOVEMBER 2015
WINDHOEK, NAMIBIA

At this conference we have been looking at the relationship between theology, politics and economics. This message reflects common themes that emerged in our conversations. One key idea is that all three—theology, politics and economics—have potential for social transformation toward a world of abundant life for all (Jn 10:10).

We have grappled with what ought to be the relationship between these three. We agreed that in Lutheran traditions, all three are intended to serve God's purposes. In fact, for Luther the economy and the body politic were theological issues. Human fallibility makes our efforts toward social transformation always less than perfect.

We identified four core features of transformative theology that inform and are informed by political and economic realities:

- Contextual:
  - Different ways of hearing God's Word
  - Different ways of relating to God's presence
  - Different ways of reflecting on and addressing diverse needs around the globe
  - Different ways of engaging with other faith traditions.

- Critical:
  - Questioning certainties—through thought, word and action

- Challenging centers of power, structures of injustice and dynamics that close down public space or exclude people from having a voice in it—through thought, word and action
- Acknowledging one's own limits, biases and self-interests—through thought, word and action.

- Creative
  - Courage to think things anew
  - Enhanced understanding of God and God's will
  - On-going dynamic development of liturgical resources and biblical hermeneutics
  - Practical solutions and alternative approaches
  - Capacity-building for bringing theology, politics and economics together for the sake of social transformation.

- Concrete
  - Speaking out and acting against injustice such as economic, gender and climate injustice.
  - Reforming structures, policies and practices.
  - Providing support, investing in education and engaging leadership.
  - Shifting curricula in theological education so that pastors and laity are equipped to engage from a faith perspective in the political and economic realms on behalf of justice.

Together these four features of theology enable it to contribute to social transformation. Sensitivity to context reveals the need for critical reflection on one's own universalizing assumptions and on the context. Critical reflection discloses that some dynamics of power and privilege need to be overthrown. This invites creativity, which in turn generates concrete actions.

Transformative theology requires and enables looking with new eyes and truth-telling about the realities that we face. Seeing with new eyes is made possible by the communion and the differences within it; deep and trusting relationships within the communion enable us to see reality through others' eyes. We are therefore profoundly grateful for the differences among us. This is precisely how a communion works and what communion is.

These reflections suggest tasks for the ongoing journey of Reformation.

1. The LWF (communion office and member churches) will build capacity within its members for bringing politics, economics, and theology together in service of social transformation according to God's vision of abundant life for all.

2. The LWF will build the communion such that member churches may share with each other how they understand and practice the public role of theology, and will provide ongoing guidance in the practice of public theology.

Reformation Day, 2015
Windhoek, Namibia

LIST OF CONTRIBUTORS

Cardoso, Nancy, Rev. Dr, is a Methodist pastor working in the ecumenical pastoral commission on land, based in Porto Alegre, Brazil

Dietrich, Stephanie, Rev. Dr, Professor, Faculty of Theology, Diaconia and Leadership Studies, VID Specialized University, Oslo, Norway

Fabiny, Tamás, Rev. Dr, Bishop of the Evangelical Lutheran Church in Hungary, Budapest, Hungary

Hallamaa, Jaana, Rev. Dr, Professor of Social Ethics, Theological Faculty, University of Helsinki, Finland

Hansen, Guillermo, Dr, Professor and Martin Luther King Jr. Chair for Justice and Christian Community, Luther Seminary, St Paul, MN, USA

Hintikka, Kaisamari, Rev. Dr, Assistant General Secretary for Ecumenical Relations and Director, Department for Theology and Public Witness, The Lutheran World Federation, Geneva, Switzerland

Jackelén, Antje, Dr, Archbishop of Uppsala and Primate of the Church of Sweden, Uppsala, Sweden

Junge, Martin, Rev. Dr, General Secretary, The Lutheran World Federation, Geneva, Switzerland

Merenlahti, Petri, Dr, Theological Adviser to the Archbishop of Turku and Finland, Finland

Mtata, Kenneth, Rev. Dr, General Secretary, Zimbabwe Council of Churches, Harare, Zimbabwe

Oberdorfer, Bernd, Dr, Professor of Systematic Theology, Augsburg University, Germany

Philip, Mary (Joy), Dr, Assistant Professor, Lutheran Global Theology and Mission, Waterloo Lutheran Seminary, Wilfrid Laurier University, Waterloo, ON, Canada

Roth, John D., Dr, Professor of History at Goshen College, director of the Institute for the Study of Global Anabaptism and editor of The Mennonite Quarterly Review, Goshen, Indiana, USA

West, Gerald O., Dr, Senior Professor, School of Religion, Philosophy, and Classics, University of KwaZulu-Natal, South Africa

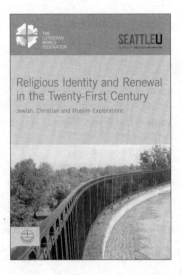